First published in 2025 by Soul Jazz Books, a division of Soul Jazz Records Ltd.

Soul Jazz Records
7 Broadwick Street London W1F 0DA
www.souljazzrecords.co.uk

Design by Adrian Self & Counter Force

Printed in Latvia
Distributed by Thames & Hudson and D.A.P.
ISBN: 978-1-9163598-4-0

FREEDOM RHYTHM & SOUND

REVOLUTIONARY JAZZ ORIGINAL COVER ART

CHAPTER TWO: JOURNEYS TO ENLIGHTENMENT

COMPILED BY GILLES PETERSON AND STUART BAKER

SOUL JAZZ BOOKS

Private. Press.

Two words that have always held a talismanic power throughout my life in and around records.

Typically used to denote records self-released (and self-funded) by an artist, or a small independent label, in limited quantities rather than by a larger music company.

But what is it about these particular records that make them so interesting to me (and to all those afflicted with the record collecting bug)?

Well, first there is the obvious record collector logic of rarity. These records were often produced with a hyper-local audience in mind - friends, family, local community, etc - and being self-funded, were necessarily made in very small runs.

So that means records that are valuable both because only a few people know about, or have them, but also on the more venal level of their financial worth.

However, what makes them more interesting to me is why they were made in the first place, and what they represent as artefacts - like a time capsule that might contain deep clues and codes about a moment and place.

Often both the quality of the recording and the artwork (and to be honest, sometimes the music itself) can be of quite variable quality, but the one consistent attribute is the raw energy of unfiltered creativity. There is also a Marxist instinct to seize the means of production as a vehicle for the truest delivery of artistic intent independent of any market logic, and in the spirit of self-expression and self-determination.

To me this unshackling of art and commerce offers the potential of true moments of magic - and I think the true power of these recordings is often the lack of any editorial A&R voice telling the music what it should or shouldn't be. Often that makes for ordinary versions that sound like the bigger records of the day, but when it hits it is pure ecstasy.

And it is this - the never-ending search for those moments - that makes private press and deep independent records so enduringly fascinating.

In a world where anything can theoretically be found at the click of a button there is still the possibility of being an intrepid explorer discovering a gem hitherto unheard. Obviously the internet has played a role in growing the fetish value of these records as well as - through finely curated compilations and books such as this one - contextualising and presenting them to a wider audience. But regardless of medium - the dopamine hit of the best new music you've not yet heard is irreplaceable.

But also it is a throwback to a pre-digital age where scarcity rather than infinite access were the thing. And one which teaches us much about some of the values we may have misplaced in the current era - independence and pure creativity as a moral, spiritual and political act. With the idea of production for and by a community at its heart. DIY is a much-used term these days - private press records are the ultimate expression of that spirit. There is much we can learn.

As someone who has run, and been around, record labels my whole life, this independent spirit is so important and flows through so much of both what I do, as well as what I am drawn to as a DJ both in the club and on the radio.

I enjoyed doing the first 'Freedom Rhythm & Sound' book (as well as 'Cuba: Music and Revolution' and 'Bossa Nova and the Rise of Brazilian Music') so much that I kept pestering Stuart to do another volume. Also because in the intervening 15 years I accumulated quite a few albums that I wanted to share.

So in this volume you will see more of the incredible artwork from independent artists and labels from the world of spiritual creative music, picking up where the first one left off, and pushing out into new directions as well as expanding the geographic reach to include records from Europe and beyond.

I hope you will enjoy leafing through the pages of this book and that it might serve both as a listening guide and an atlas for discovery.

Gilles Peterson

FREEDOM, RHYTHM & SOUND
Introduction

This is the second volume of revolutionary record cover designs. The album covers appeared on self-released, private-press editions, or on albums released on predominantly independent record labels. They frame the developments in jazz music in the 1960s, 70s, 80s and beyond, that took place outside the commercial environment of the mainstream music industry.

The artwork often reflects a radical political and social agenda informed by the larger Civil Rights Movement of the 1960s, as well as a spiritual awareness, and a singular search for musical and personal freedoms. Graphic and highly individual designs, often in just one or two colours, perfectly captured the spirit of the music they contained. From raw DIY aesthetics to lyrical and poetic illustrations, the designs are always bold, strikingly graphic and possess a beauty all of their own.

This book features hundreds of unique, beautiful, rare and idiosyncratic images. In addition, it includes sections of artwork that appeared on records from related areas including African-American poetry in the USA, civil rights and black power speeches, and the early roots of this new music. All these, in one way or another, contributed to shape and influence the world of radical jazz from the 1960s onwards.

The book should be seen as an accompaniment to the first Freedom, Rhythm and Sound, where, aside from many more record designs, you will also find text on The Art Ensemble of Chicago, Sun Ra, John and Alice Coltrane, Mary Lou Williams, Strata-East, Flying Dutchman, ESP-Disk, India Navigation and more.

This new volume documents a second chapter in the evolution of radical jazz. Essentially a diasporic journey of enlightenment a number of African-American jazz musicians embarked upon when they travelled to Europe at the end of the 1960s, having become frustrated at the slow progress of systemic change in the USA. In Europe they found both a willing audience ready to hear their radical music and a nascent independent recording industry, eager to document the sound.

The book illustrates how this experience empowered them as artists. This, in turn, affected their relationship with the music industry on their return to the USA, leading to a wealth of new independent and private-press record companies in the 1970s all focussed on jazz as an art form (as opposed to an entertainment). These artists also impacted on local musicians and the music industry in Europe and there are sections in this book featuring European independent labels and European private-pressing releases that came into existence as a direct consequence of this voyage.

Finally there is a rebirth. Since the first volume of Freedom, Rhythm and Sound was published many lost and rare independent jazz records have been made available once more. Artists that appeared in the first volume have continued to make new music. Younger artists have also created new music that extends the lineage of these original radical artists. A snapshot of this new landscape is captured at the end section of this book.

Civil Rights and Black Power

The impact the Civil Rights and Black Power Movements had on the evolution of jazz music from the 1960s onwards cannot be overstated. And few records announced the intention of jazz music to march side-by-side along the path of the Civil Rights Movement more than Max Roach's 'We Insist! Freedom Now Suite', released on Candid Records in 1961. This album featured the proud faces of three men demonstrating their opposition to segregation in the United States by staging a sit-in at a diner lunch counter, where African-Americans were not allowed to sit according to segregationist laws.

Nina Simone, Duke Ellington, John Coltrane, Miles Davis, Cannonball Adderley, Louis Armstrong, Max Roach, Charles Mingus and many other jazz musicians contributed to the civil rights cause - either creating music that reflected the struggles and ideals of the movement or, more prosaically, playing at fundraising events in aid of the cause.

'Jazz … takes the hardest realities of life and puts them into music, only to come out with some new hope or sense of triumph.' Thus spoke Martin Luther King in his essay on the importance of jazz, written at the request of the organisers of the Berlin Jazz Festival in September 1964. The festival featured performances by, among others, Miles Davis, Roland Kirk and Sister Rosetta Tharpe.

Malcolm X and the Black Power Movement was to have no less of an effect on jazz music in the second-half of the 1960s, directly inspiring the agenda of proto-rap groups such as The Last Poets and Watts Prophets, but more generally inspiring a sense of self-determination, pride and liberation within the psyche of soul and jazz musicians, and indeed all African-Americans. Songs such as James Brown's 'Say It Loud, I'm Black and I'm Proud' and Gil Scott-Heron's 'The Revolution Will Not Be Televised' illustrated these ideals, attempting to redress frustrations felt by continued racial discrimination despite the advances of the Civil Rights Movement.

Perhaps nothing exemplified this more than the white supremacist firebombing that killed four black children inside the 16th Street Baptist Church in Birmingham, Alabama on September 15, 1963. In the months that followed John Coltrane composed 'Alabama'. The song's melodic line is based on Martin Luther King's eulogy at the service for three of the victims, Addie Mae Collins, Carol Denise McNair, and Cynthia Diane Wesley. A separate service was held for the fourth victim, Carole Robertson. Nina Simone wrote 'Mississippi Goddam' following the bombing as well as the recent gunning down of civil rights activist Medgar Evers in Mississippi. Expressing frustration at the slow rate of change she sang;

Desegregation (too slow)
Mass participation (too slow)
Reunification (too slow)
Do things gradually (too slow)
But bring more tragedy (too slow)
Why don't you see it? Why don't you feel it?

I don't know, I don't know
You don't have to live next to me
Just give me my equality
Everybody knows about Mississippi
Everybody knows about Alabama
Everybody knows about Mississippi, goddamn
That's it!'

Black Arts Movement

Black Power also gave rise to the Black Arts Movement which aimed to use art as a tool for social and political change, promoting black self-determination and challenging racial inequality. The movement emphasised the importance of black identity, history, and culture, and sought to create a distinct cultural space for black people.

Through the development of the Black Arts Movement, jazz musicians saw their work as part of a wider cultural sphere that included dance, theatre, poetry and more. Writers and poets such as Langston Hughes, James Baldwin, Amira Baraka, Nikki Giovanni, Sarah Webster Fabio, Haki R. Madhubuti and others helped inform this, often interacting with jazz music and helping to create a direct lineage that led from Gil Scott-Heron and The Last Poets to the birth of hip-hop at the end of the 1970s.

A number of musicians collectives were also inspired by the Black Arts Movement. The first of these was the Association for the Advancement of Creative Musicians (AACM) in Chicago, whose mission was dedicated to 'nurturing, performing, and recording serious, original music.' The organisation was founded in 1965 by pianist Muhal Richard Abrams, pianist Jodie Christian, drummer Steve McCall, and composer Phil Cohran. The idea for the collective came out of Abrams' earlier Experimental Band which had been active since 1961. AACM members include The Art Ensemble of Chicago, Anthony Braxton, Henry Threadgill, Leroy Jenkins, Kahil El'Zabar, Chico Freeman, Amina Claudine Myers, Wadada Leo smith and others. With the slogan 'Great Black Music, Ancient to the Future', the AACM remains a mainstay of creative music sixty years on. Other music collectives in the USA that set up at this time included the Black Artists Group in St Louis, Tribe in Detroit and the Underground Musicians Association (UGMA)/Union of God's Musicians and Artists Ascension (UGMAA) in Los Angeles (for more on these associations see the first Freedom, Rhythm and Sound).

The successes of the Civil Rights and Black Power Movements meant that artists began to take more control of their musical paths: where they chose to perform, what music they played, with some asserting control over their master recordings (although this phenomena remained a rare occurrence and it was not until the 1970s that artist-owned recordings became more commonplace).

The First Private-Press and Independent Record Labels

Private-press records were usually manufactured in very small quantities, self-distributed, often solely at artists' own concerts, or on consignment in local stores. These records were labours of love - art rather than commerce - sitting outside the ruthlessly commercial world of the major music industry. Musicians and designers alike were free to express themselves in a way that was previously not possible. This creative freedom resulted in some of the most striking and revolutionary music - and record sleeve artworks.

Stepping outside of the mainstream was almost total for some jazz musicians in the 1970s. Some artists chose to perform in galleries and musician-owned, or rented, loft spaces, thus avoiding unscrupulous nightclub owners and their practices. Radical jazz music became a communal and collective activity – both in terms of improvisatory technique and also in the role of this music in society. Rejecting the notion of music as a commercial venture, concerts were often organised as benefits for community projects. In a democratic gesture, artists also chose to minimise the separation or barriers between stage and audience.

Most of the artwork designs featured in this book date from the 1970s and early 1980s. Artists who released music on their own small, private-press labels, or with independent labels, had creative freedom, in a way that precious few signed to a major label enjoyed. But to understand the context of how this new more democratic industry environment came about, we first need to take a step back to both the first African-American owned record business and the first African-American artist-led companies:

W.C. Handy, one of the most influential songwriters in the United States, and his songwriting partner Harry Pace, founded the publishers Pace and Handy Music Company in Memphis in 1912. While Pace noted the growing rise of the phonograph, Handy preferred writing and selling sheet music and the partnership dissolved amicably a few years later. Pace moved to New York and formed Black Swan Records in Harlem in 1921, the first widely-distributed African-American owned record company. With Fletcher Henderson as recording director the label released scores of blues, gospel and classical records.

But Black Swan was unfortunately short-lived, declaring bankruptcy in 1923 when it was sold to Paramount Records. America would have to wait almost three decades for any other significant African-American jazz artists to own their own record companies. This was achieved (separately) by three of the hippest and most successful bebop artists in the early 1950s: Dizzy Gillespie, Charles Mingus and Max Roach.

Dizzy Gillespie, and his business partner Dave Usher, founded Dee Gee Records in Detroit in 1951. The label was initially set-up to release Gillespie's own material but soon branched out to release music by friends and colleagues, including Milt Jackson, Shelly Manne, Kenny Clarke and others. Dee Gee released the first ever track by soul singer Jackie Wilson (as Sonny Wilson, singing 'Danny Boy'). Their first release was Gillespie's debut recording of the Afro-Cuban classic 'Tin Tin Deo' (labelled as 'Tin Tin Daeo'), written by arranger Gil Fuller and Cuban percussionist Chano Pozo. In Gillespie's group, on this recording, was a young John Coltrane, as well as Kenny Burrell and Milt Jackson. Struggling financially, Dee Gee closed in 1953, and was acquired by Savoy Records in 1956.

One year after Dee Gee Records was formed, Charles Mingus and Max Roach established their own record label, when along with Mingus' wife Celia, they created Debut Records. This allowed them to retain artistic control over their own work and circumvent the restrictions of the major record companies. As well as their own material they released music by Bud Powell, Miles Davis, Hank Mobley, Paul Bley and others. The label folded a little over five years later when Charles and Celia Mingus divorced in 1958. Charles Mingus later gave his share to his ex-wife as a wedding gift when she married Saul Zaentz. Zaentz at the time worked at Fantasy Records, one of the largest independent jazz labels. Zaentz became president of Fantasy in 1967 and later acquired a portfolio of other important jazz record labels including Prestige (1971), Riverside (1972) and Milestone (1972).

Gillespie, Mingus and Roach were well-known jazz artists with already established recording careers prior to setting up their own companies. But it was an outsider to the mainstream music recording industry who created the template for artist-led record labels. Ihnfinity Incorporated first came into existence in Chicago in 1954, and was officially registered in 1957 by Sunny Blount, aka Sun Ra, along with his manager Alton Abraham, James Bryant and Almeter Hayden (Alton Abraham's sister).

Out of this company came El Saturn Records, perhaps the defining private-press record label of all. Sun Ra was unable to find any interest from major record companies and El Saturn was created to make his music available to the public. Ihnfinity Incorporated's activities included arranging concerts as well as printing spiritually and educationally uplifting pamphlets.

Sun Ra had owned his own recording equipment since the 1930s; first a Brush Development Company's 'Sound Mirror' wire tape recorder he had purchased in 1937, then an Ampex paper tape recorder in 1948. Some of his early recordings made on these machines were eventually released on El Saturn. El Saturn Records were printed in small runs, sometimes with hand-painted or silk-screened sleeves and sold by hand primarily at Sun Ra concerts.

This early assertion of control can be seen as a transitionary step in the evolution of jazz musician from entertainer to artist. It took a revolution in sound for the next phase to take place at the tail end of the 1950s when African-American jazz artists began to 'deconstruct' jazz itself - pivoting away from the increasingly complex sound of be-bop, complete with its aesthetic of instrumental virtuosity and on stage 'cutting contests' (where musicians tried to outdo one another's solos), and searching instead for a more collective and spiritual understanding of the meaning of jazz.

The New Jazz

Miles Davis' 'Kind of Blue' was released on Colombia Records on August 17, 1959. Featuring John Coltrane, Bill Evans, Cannonball Adderley, Paul Chambers and Jimmy Cobb, the record was a reaction to this increasingly complex musical form. Davis chose instead to experiment with the idea of modality, essentially freeing musicians to stretch out and improvise without the need to be conscious of relentless chord changes. Davis had first explored this idea the previous year with his track 'Milestones'. This concept of modality created a new pathway for jazz that was then expanded upon by artists such as John Coltrane, Pharoah Sanders, Herbie Hancock, Davis himself and others throughout the 1960s.

In the same year that Miles Davis released 'Kind of Blue', Ornette Coleman recorded 'The Shape of Jazz to Come' on Atlantic Records, presaging the arrival of Coleman's ground-breaking 'Free Jazz: A Collective Improvisation' album in 1961. Abandoning traditional ideas of harmony, tonality, fixed rhythms and chord changes in favour of collective improvisation, Coleman became the pied-piper for 'free jazz' – spontaneous, chaotic, sometimes hard to listen to, angry, spiritual.

The new music had arrived and artists began to add layers to its meaning. Afro-centricity became another key element to the new jazz as Art Blakey, Randy Weston, Yusef Lateef and others began to explore their links to Africa, for the first time tracing a lineage from the roots of African-American jazz back to its origins.

As the 1960s progressed, artists including John Coltrane, Pharoah Sanders and Yusef Lateef also added a deeply spiritual element into the musical equation; jazz music became a way to communicate on a higher consciousness with god, nature and the world. Sun Ra took this one stage further, expanding musical vibrations that travelled the astral highways of space from his Saturn base.

These four new pathways – modality, free jazz, spirituality, afro-centricity - together with the influence of the Civil Rights and Black Power Movements, and lastly a willingness to experiment with other forms, established the sound of the new modern and radical jazz.

The first labels to release this new music were already established large independent jazz labels - Blue Note, Atlantic, Riverside, Contemporary and Savoy. Impulse! Records, founded by Creed Taylor in 1960, became a major force in modern jazz after signing John Coltrane in 1962. Coltrane, with producer Bob Thiele, released over a dozen albums for Impulse! in the five years before his death, and ushered in much of the new wave of jazz, including Pharoah Sanders, Archie Shepp, Alice Coltrane and others.

But it was a new upstart label, ESP-Disk, that was the first to focus solely on free jazz, also known as the 'new thing' or simply the 'new music'. With its slogan 'The artists alone decide what you will hear on their ESP-Disk', label owner Bernard Stollman recorded many of these first wave of free jazz musicians including Albert Ayler, Sun Ra, Sonny Simmons, Frank Wright, Ornette Coleman, Giuseppi Logan, Burton Greene and Steve Lacy. Most of these artists were signed in one go after Stollman attended the 'October Revolution in Jazz', a four-day festival organised by the musician Bill Dixon, held at the Cellar Café in New York from Oct 1-4 1964. Dixon also created The Jazz Composers Guild and, later, a non-profit organisation called the Jazz Composers Orchestra Association Inc. (JCOA).

With limited connections to the major music industry, Stollman took his business model from Folkways Records, probably the first 'world' music label, a cottage industry founded by Moses Asch and Marian Distler in 1948. Folkways specialised in 'ethnographic' recordings from around the world, edited by anthropologist Harold Courlander. The label was also steeped in folk and southern music, recording Woody Guthrie, Pete Seeger, Leadbelly and many others, which put it at the centre of the American folk music revival in the 1960s.

Many of Folkways recordings were extremely specialised and sold in very small quantities, making it hard for the label to be economically viable. Despite this Asch managed to keep the label running by amassing a huge catalogue of recordings (over 2,000 albums from 1948-1986 when he died) and meticulous book-keeping. Folkways releases could be pressed up in small runs and were sleeved in generic black card sleeves to which stickered artwork was then attached. Stollman had done some legal work at Folkways, and was impressed at how Asch managed to keep the decidedly non-commercial record company afloat and attempted to emulate this, developing a catalogue that left the artist in charge of the music and essentially free from commercial concerns.

In September 1965, ESP-Disk released a dozen titles simultaneously including Pharoah Sanders, The New York Art Quartet, Albert Ayler and Ornette Coleman. Three years later the label was essentially closed down. According to Stollman they were victims of either (or both) bootlegging or political interference (for more on ESP see the first edition of Freedom, Rhythm and Sound).

From the 1960s onwards, all of these radical jazz artists - Sun Ra, John Coltrane, Pharoah Sanders, The Art Ensemble of Chicago, Ornette Coleman and others - helped reshape the cultural landscape of African-American jazz musicians in the USA, pushing the boundaries of what jazz music could be, as well as fundamentally changing the role of a jazz musician in society. While re-evaluating their position, many artists reflected on the traditional relationship between musician and record company, and instead chose to self-produce and manufacture their own work.

While the major label recording industry still represented the biggest names in jazz - Coltrane, Miles, Duke Ellington, Herbie Hancock, Dizzy Gillespie and so on - many African-American jazz artists during this period (roughly 1960-80) led active musical careers while never becoming a part of the mainstream. For some, the offer was never on the table, but for many this was an active and political rejection of the commercial terms of the recording industry.

The 1970s was to prove a fertile era for both artist-owned bespoke record companies, and new independent record labels alike, many of whom had learnt from the mistakes of the major recording industry and offered a more respectful relationship with the artists that chose to work with them.

New labels such as Muse, Black Jazz, Inner City, India Navigation, Delmark all prioritised artistic freedom ahead of commercial success. Labels such as Strata-East, Tribe and Strata were all artist-owned.

In regard to the major jazz labels, Blue Note Records - powerhouse of hard bop in the 1950s and 60s - was acquired by Liberty Records in 1965, which was itself sold to United Artists in 1972. Blue Note's founder Alfred Lion retired in 1967, designer Reid Miles left around the same time and A&R Duke Pearson left a short time after.

This essentially left Blue Note at the start of the 1970s as a re-issue label for its earlier catalogue. This did not change until around 1972 when new executive producer, George Butler, brought in the production team Larry and Fonze Mizell and their Sky High Productions which helped create a highly successful commercial jazz funk sound for of a number of Blue Note artists including Donald Byrd and Bobbi Humphrey, far away from the non-mainstream sensibilities of the records that feature here.

Impulse!, another major label, fared much better in the early 1970s. John Coltrane's seminal early 1960s releases, and those of the Coltrane musical family that he brought into the label, had ushered in the first wave of modern jazz. His death in 1967 and the subsequent departure of Coltrane's producer, Bob Thiele, the following year, would have signalled the end for most labels, let alone 'the house that Trane built'.

However the arrival of producer Ed Michel at Impulse! to replace Thiele proved fruitful. At the start of the 1970s Michel set up a meeting between Sun Ra and Alton Abraham, Ra's business manager and partner in El Saturn Records, and ABC, the parent company of Impulse! A deal was struck to license recordings from El Saturn Records. Michel also took over production for Impulse's core artists including Pharoah Sanders, Archie Shepp, Albert Ayler and Alice Coltrane. Michel did this respectfully, and, in so doing, gave the label continuity.

Producer Bob Thiele, meanwhile, set up his own label, Flying Dutchman with major distribution from Atlantic Records. Through Coltrane, Thiele had been involved with the most important, radical jazz music of the 1960s and intended to do the same thing in his new vehicle, setting out his stall immediately with important cutting-edge jazz releases by Leon Thomas, Horace Tapscott and others. Flying Dutchman also released a steady stream of overtly political civil rights and Black Power commentators and poets including Stanley Crouch ('Ain't No Ambulances for No Nigguhs Tonight'), H Rap Brown ('SNCC Rap') and Angela Davis ('Soul and Soledad'). Few people could have believed that polemical political speeches or poetry could become a success, but, in 1970, Thiele released Gil Scott-Heron's debut 'Small Talk at 125th and Lenox'.

This became the first in a series of classic albums on the label, and proved Thiele's faith in the commercial viability of these revolutionary areas of discourse.

Of the other majors, Colombia Records was the most successful label at selling jazz in the 1970s. First with 'electric period' Miles Davis and then Herbie Hancock, Colombia showed that jazz could reach the rock market and garner the large commercial sales that came with it.

Atlantic Records, the home of soul music in the 1960s, and hard rock in the 1970s, focussed its jazz division primarily on soul jazz artists - Dave Newman, Eddie Harris, Herbie Mann, Les McCann - but also housed more experimental artists such as Roland Kirk and Yusef Lateef.

But the options for jazz artists in America to work with these established labels remained relatively small and musicians had little option at the start of the 1970s except to do it themselves or work with the relatively small number of independent labels. In response to this musical landscape, and the continued inequalities felt by African-American musicians in their own society, artists began to look further afield.

Europe

Many African-American jazz artists left America to live or work in Europe in the 1960s: Ornette Coleman, Albert Ayler, Cecil Taylor, Eric Dolphy, Nathan Davis, Art Farmer, Horace Parlan, Duke Jordan, Kenny Clarke, Johnny Griffin, Ben Webster, Kenny Drew and Oscar Pettiford, Nina Simone, The Art Ensemble of Chicago, Don Cherry, Mal Waldron, Archie Shepp and others. On arrival in Europe, these performers found fresh, eager audiences who instinctively bestowed a long-strived for respect upon them.

For many musicians the first port of call was Paris, second home to a small but significant amount of African-American cultural figures throughout the twentieth century. Dancer Josephine Baker, literary figures James Baldwin, Chester Himes, Langston Hughes, Richard Wright, black intellectuals such as W.E. Dubois all made Paris their home for extended periods of time. Here they found less overt racism and their art more culturally valued than back home.

In autumn 1968, after a farewell performance at the Unitarian Church in Evanston, Illinois, The Art Ensemble, comprised of The Association for the Advancement of Creative Musicians members Lester Bowie, Joseph Jarman, Malachi Favors and Roscoe Mitchell travelled to Paris. They based themselves at the Théâtre du Vieux Colombier. On the advice of the local promoter 'of Chicago' was added to their group name. They soon found themselves recording for a host of French record companies including BYG Records, Saravah, Galloway, Decca and America Records, as well as Freedom in the UK. They also appeared in, and scored, the music to the nouvelle vague film 'Les Stances a Sophie' by director Moshé Mizrahi, the soundtrack released on Pathé in France (and Nessa in the USA), and on which they were joined by drummer Don Moye and vocalist Fontella Bass.

The commercial possibilities of recording forward-thinking African-American jazz music was not lost on a number of local producers across Europe. The immediate consequence of the diasporic journey of these journeymen jazz musicians was the establishment of a network of significant new independent European record labels, eager for the chance to work with these important artists. And an added bonus was that many of these artists were not tied to major label contracts in the USA.

New European record labels that opened often followed a start-up template of releasing new music by ex-pat African-American artists and introducing younger European artists. These companies included ECM, Enja and Japo in Germany, Steeplechase in Denmark, Horo, Black Saint and Soul Note in Italy, Timeless in the Netherlands, Black Lion and Freedom in Britain and others. Many of these record companies still exist today. Many other European artist-owned or private-press labels set up during this period, similarly inspired by the music and sensibilities of the ground-breaking African- American artists who came to Europe.

Returning to the USA in the 1970s

In 1972, The Art Ensemble of Chicago returned to the USA with other artists following later. Despite the relatively short lapse in time, artists found a different social and cultural landscape to that which they had left. The demands of the Civil Rights and Black Power Movement had, to a certain degree, been achieved. Similarly 'free jazz' musicians were now accepted into the mainstream - that same year Ornette Coleman released 'Skies of America' performed with the London Symphony Orchestra. New artist-focussed independent labels like Strata-East, Muse, Tribe and Black Jazz Records were established.

Forward-thinking jazz artists found themselves freer to explore their creative artistry, having successfully renegotiated their relationship with the USA record industry, having decided on their own terms whether to work from within or exist outside. This became a golden period for conscious jazz musicians; independent labels thrived and many artists were able to reach an audience through releasing their own music.

Loft Spaces

In the mid-1970s, live spaces similarly became contested grounds for political and social change. The maltreatment of musicians by corrupt nightclub owners had long been a source of frustration. A number of jazz musicians in New York decided to open up their own mixed-usage live/work spaces, lofts and cheap rent warehouses as places for experimental live jazz, dance and performance. Usually charging a small admission price, with little barriers between artist and audience, these new locations became 'community spaces', sacred ground for creative spirits.

The first of these was Ornette Coleman's Artist House at 131 Prince Street, a space he acquired in April 1968, having bought shares in a co-op that purchased a seven-story building. Coleman had two floors, each 3,500 square foot, one of which he lived in and the other he used as his work space. At first this was used as a rehearsal room for his band but in 1970 he opened it up as an informal concert room for like-minded jazz musicians and an art gallery. Artists House stayed open until 1974 and Coleman moved out shortly afterwards.

More loft spaces sprang up in New York in the mid-1970s including Sam and Bea Rivers' Studio Rivbea, Rashied Ali's Studio 77, later Ali's Alley, Stanley Crouch and David Murray's Studio Infinity, John Fischer's Environ and others.

During this period many members from the countrywide musical collectives came to New York, creating a new vibrant and avant-garde 'loft jazz' scene. These included, from Chicago, AACM members Muhal Richard Abrams, Anthony Braxton, Kalaparusha Maurice McIntyre, Lester Bowie, Amina Claudine Myers, Henry Threadgill, Steve McCall, Fred Hopkins, Chico Freeman, Malachi Thompson; from St Louis, BAG members Charles 'Bobo' Shaw, Oliver Lake, Julius Hemphill, Hamiet Bluiett, Joseph Bowie; and from Los Angeles, UGMAA members Arthur Blythe, David Murray, and Butch Morris.

Loft spaces were run by jazz musicians like cooperatives, the music performed in them focussed on continuing the pathways first explored by the artists Sun Ra, John Coltrane, Albert Ayler, Archie Shepp and Pharoah Sanders at the start of the 1960s, prioritising spiritual and artistic expression over any commercial ideas.

New York's loft jazz scene lasted until the end of the 1970s when rent hikes led to many of these locations shutting their doors. Into the 1980s many radical African-American jazz artists dispersed once more, performing and recording anywhere in the world, in similar considered fashion to their forebears, continuing to prioritise creative and personal integrity over commerce.

So how does the narrative of this story end? There was no loss in faith in the righteous path of musical and spiritual exploration. No crushing by the corporate giants. No selling out. Instead it was a technological development that brought a close to the vibrant age of private-press and independent jazz recordings during this era. In 1979, Sony and Philips set up a joint task force of engineers to design a new 'digital audio disc'. By 1988 CD sales in the USA had overtaken LPs, reaching their peak at the end of the 1990s just as streaming services arrived, which over time became the new dominant 'digital' way for music to be consumed. Vinyl lay dormant, awaiting its rebirth in the next century.

And while a few put forward the notion that listening to music digitally was preferable to analogue, no one claimed that looking at a five-inch illustration behind plastic, or a two-inch digital thumbnail, was in any way an advancement in the way we can view the beautiful and righteous imagery contained within the album designs featured here, many of which have remained hidden to all but the few.

Stuart Baker

BROTHER MALACHI FAVORS MAGOUSTOUS Natural & Spiritual **AECO Records** 1978
Cover Artwork by Kenneth Hunter **Typography by** Chaga Olamina

CLIFFORD JORDAN QUARTET Night Of The Mark VII **MUSE RECORDS** 1975
Illustration by Stanley Ray **Cover Artwork by** Sandra Williams

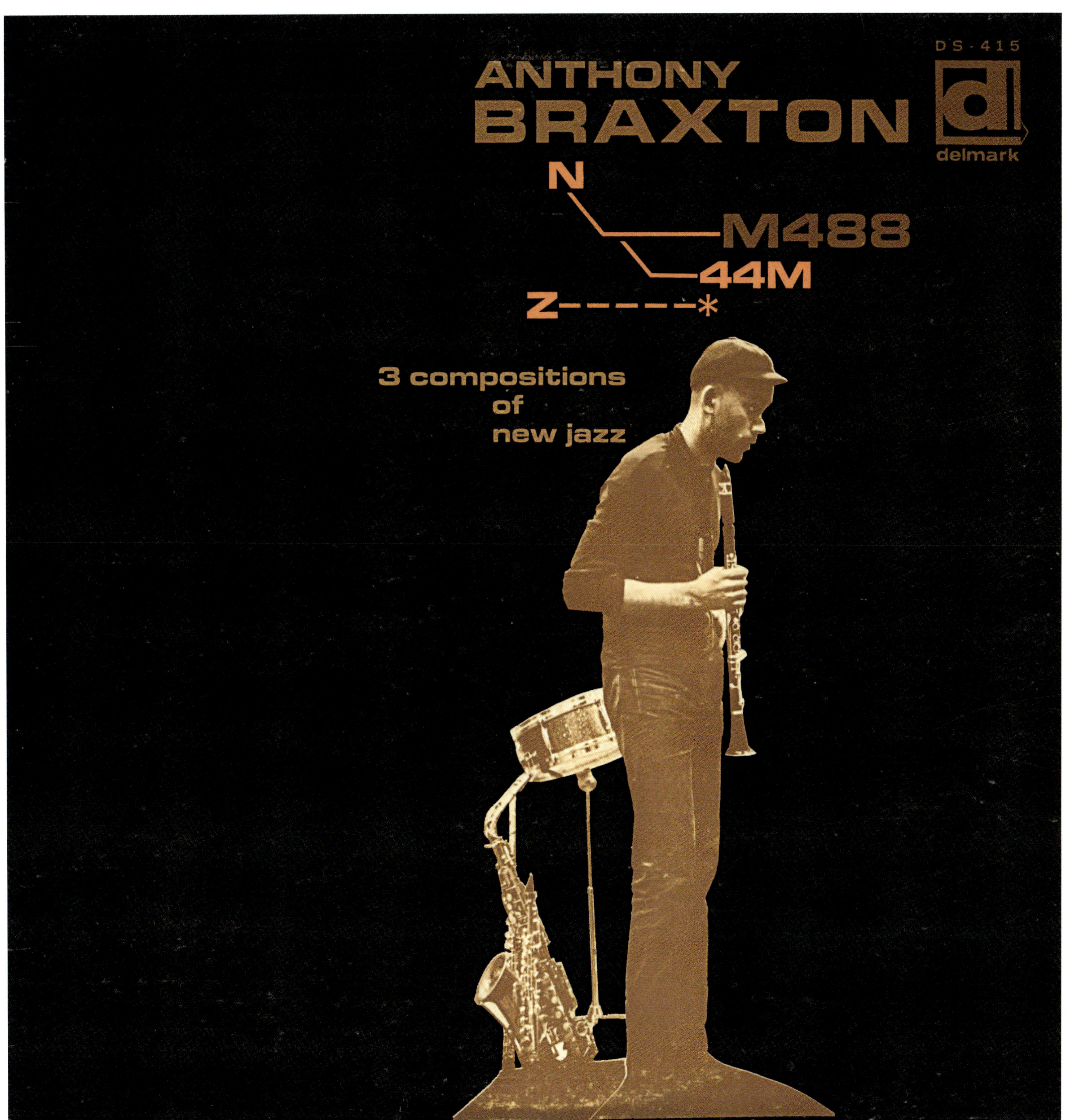

ANTHONY BRAXTON 3 Compositions Of New Jazz **DELMARK RECORDS** 1968

JEROME COOPER QUINTET Outer and Interactions **About Time Records** 1988
Cover Artwork & Drawing by Beth Cummins **Album Design by** Judith Ziegler

CHA CHA SHAW Kingdom Come **Folkways Records** 1979

RAY PIZZI Appassionato **P.Z. Records** 1975
Photography by Phil Teele

JAYNE CORTEZ Celebrations And Solitudes **Strata East Records** 1974
Photography by Mel Edwards

Library of Congress Catalog Card Number: R 65-2866
R 65-2867

THE GIUSEPPI LOGAN QUARTET The Giuseppi Logan Quartet **ESP-Disk** 1966
Cover Artwork by Howard Bernstein

SAM RIVERS Hues **Impulse!** 1975
Illustration by Ed Scarisbrick **Photography by** Philip Melnick

CARLOS GARNETT Journey To Enlightenment **Muse Records** 1974
Design and painting by Ron Warwell

FRANK HATCHETT Spirit Free and New Horizons **Statler Records** 1980

SUN RA Days of Happiness **El Saturn Records** 1979
(Photocopied hand-made sleeve)

BLACK SPIRITS
FESTIVAL OF NEW BLACK POETS IN AMERICA

IMAMU AMIRI BARAKA (LE ROI JONES) □ THE ORIGINAL LAST POETS

JOHARI AMINI
CLARENCE MAJOR
NORMAN JORDAN
KALI
JACKIE EARLEY

ASKI MOHAMMAD TOURE
DAVID HENDERSON
STANLEY CROUCH
LARRY NEAL
AMUS MOORE

VARIOUS ARTISTS / IMAMU AMIRI BARAKA Black Spirits: Festival Of New Black Poets In America **BLACK FORUM** 1972
Photography by Jim Britt

THE BILL DIXON ORCHESTRA Intents And Purposes **RCA Victor** 1967
Photography by David B Hecht

CECIL TAYLOR Student Studies **BYG Records** 1973

GARY BARTZ Another Earth **Milestone** 1969
Cover Artwork by John Murello **Photography by** Charles Stewart

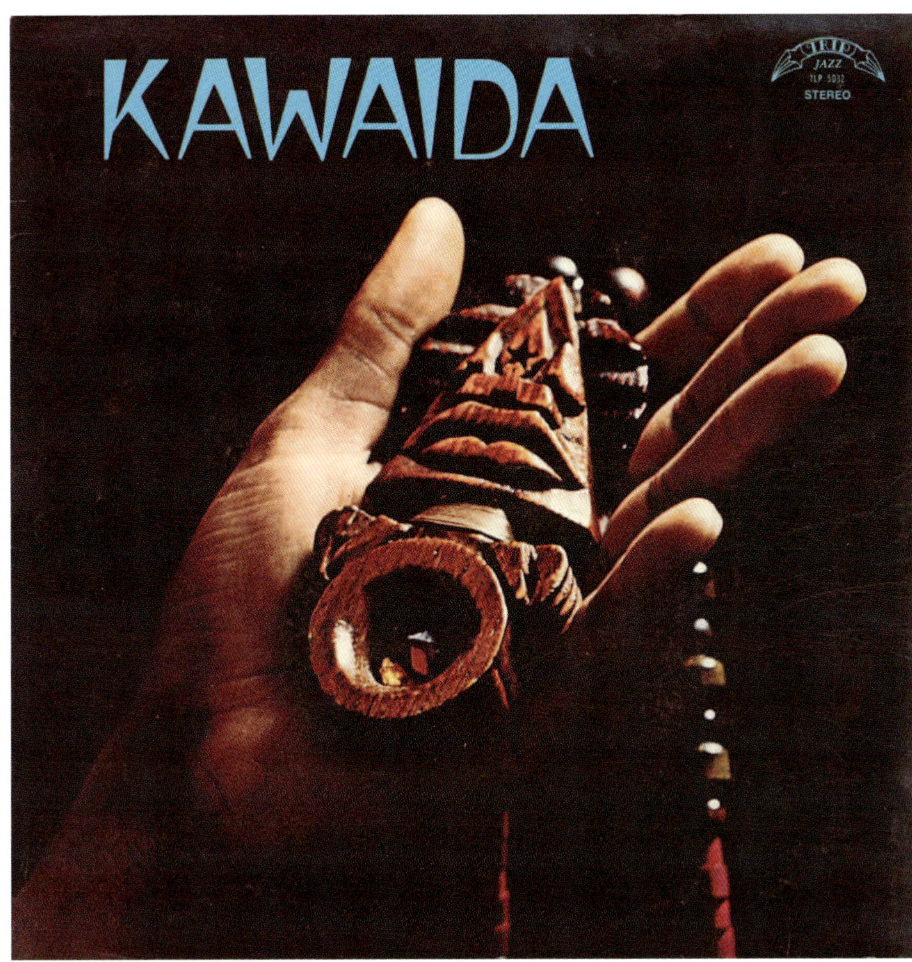

KUUMBA-TOUDIE HEATH Kawaida **Trip** 1974 (Originally issued on O'Be Records, 1970)
Photography by Martin Bough **Art Direction** Peter Weir

CREATIVE CONSTRUCTION COMPANY Creative Construction Company Vol II **Muse Records** 1976
Art Direction & Cover Painting by P Givens **Cover Artwork by** Doug Dunn

GRACAN MONCUR III Aco Dei De Madrugada (One Morning I Waked Up Very Early) / New Africa **BYG RECORDS** 1971
Design by Dominique Broc **Photography by** Jacques Bisceglia, Nadja Pictures, Philippe Gras

POETS AND WRITERS

As Jazz came under the wider umbrella of the Black Arts Movement in the mid-1960s, musicians aligned themselves closely with dancers, playwrights, painters and sculptors, writers and poets, all of whom were infusing their art with shared values of racial pride, self-determination, economic empowerment, and political and cultural autonomy.

In fact, this cross-pollinating of art forms, especially the connection between poetry and jazz, went back much further in time to the Harlem Renaissance, the intellectual and cultural movement of African-American music, art and literature centred around Harlem, New York in the 1920s and 1930s. The Harlem Renaissance had been fuelled by the Great Migration of African-Americans from the South.

Langston Hughes, born in 1901, was a major figure in the Harlem Renaissance. Other key figures in this movement included Zora Neale Hurston, Wallace Thurman, Claude McKay and Duke Ellington.

Hughes was a polymath - poet, social activist, novelist and playwright - and played an innovative role in the creation of what he called 'jazz poetry'. 'The Negro Speaks of Rivers' (with its opening line 'I've known rivers, ancient as the world, and older than the flow of human blood in human veins') became Hughes' signature poem, collected in his first book of poetry, 'The Weary Blues', first published in 1926.

At the end of the 1920s, Hughes travelled to the southern states with Zora Neale Thurston studying local customs and folklore. This resulted in 'The Book of Negro Folklore' and 'Not Without Laughter', a novel about the singer Bessie Smith, who Hughes and Thurston had encountered on the trip.

In his novels, Hughes wrote about working-class African-American life. His work discussed racial consciousness, cultural nationalism and a global black aesthetic that made him an inspirational figure in the Black Arts Movement. He drew upon jazz and folk rhythms as the basis of his poetry of racial pride - and jazz music played a large part in his work.

In 1958, Hughes narrated 'The Story of Jazz' for Folkways Records, based on his book for children, 'The First Book of Jazz' (1954). He recorded 'The Glory of Negro History' a year later, again for Folkways. In 1958, he voiced 'The Weary Blues' on record for MGM. In 1961, he wrote lyrics for Randy Weston's ground-breaking album 'Uhuru Afrika (Freedom Africa)' featuring Yusef Lateef, Sahib Shihab, Charlie Persip, Budd Johnson and others. Hughes continued to record material through the 1960s, up until his death in 1967.

Posthumously released albums included Hughes' recording of 'Black Verse – 12 Modes for Jazz' (1969), based on his 1961 poem 'Ask Your Mama: 12 Moods for Jazz', in which he discusses the relationship between jazz and poetry. The poem uses the template of the 12-bar blues as a structural framework for its twelve sections. Hughes included musical notation in the poem's margins, inviting a performance style that blends spoken word and music.

Hughes first performed the poem at the

LANGSTON HUGHES The Weary Blues With.. **MGM Records** 1958
Design by Fran Scott

THE WATTS PROPHETS Rappin' Black In A White World **Ala Records 1971**
Design by Howard Goldstein **Photography by** Dominic Belmonte

ELAINE BROWN Elaine Brown **BLACK FORUM** 1973

RUBY DEE AND OSSIE DAVIS The Poetry Of Langston Hughes **Caedmon Records** 1969
Illustration by Gregorio Prestopino

CAMILLE YARBROUGH The Iron Pot Cooker **Vanguard** 1975
Photography by Sue Greene

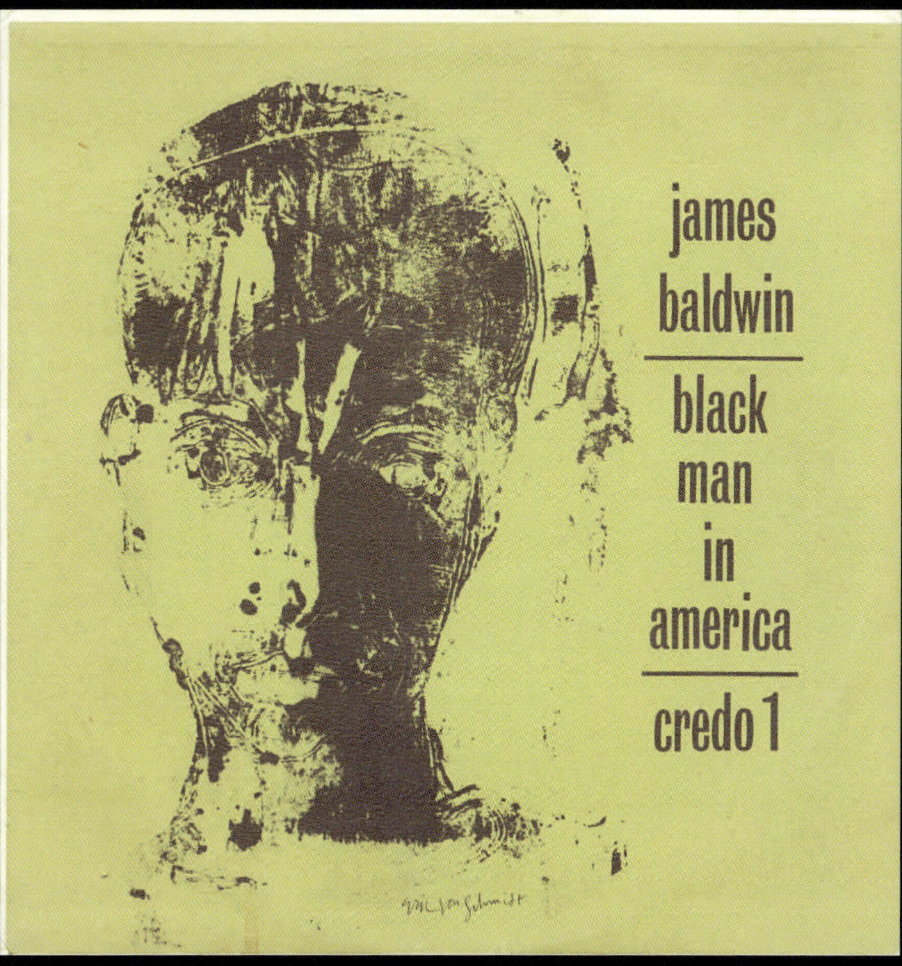

JAMES BALDWIN Black Man In America (An Interview by Studs Terkel) **Credo 1** 1962
Design by Eric Von Schmidt **Photography by** Roy Hyrkin

Newport Jazz Festival. The poem explores the black experience, and the legacy of colonialism. The album was released as part of Buddah Records' Black America series which also featured James Baldwin's 'The Struggle' and two albums by radio DJ and historian Nathaniel Montague, the man who coined the phrase 'Burn Baby, Burn', which became a famous refrain in the Watts Riots in 1965.

In 1970, Motown's subsidiary spoken word Black Forum label released an album by Langston Hughes and Margaret Danner called 'Writers of the Revolution'. Other figures in this series included Martin Luther King, Stokely Carmichael, Imamu Amiri Baraka and Ossie Davis.

African-American poet, activist, publisher, writer and performer Jayne Cortez was married to Ornette Coleman from 1954 to 1964. In 1964, she founded the Watts Repertory Theater Company, and served as artistic director until 1970. She published her first poetry collection in 1969 and described herself as a 'jazz poet'.

Two years later she founded her own publishing company, Bola Press. On her first album 'Celebrations and Solitudes', released on Strata-East Records in 1974, Cortez performed her poetry accompanied by bassist Richard Davis.

At the end of the decade Bola Press also began to release her records, backed by The Firespitters, an electro-funk jazz outfit which included her son, Denardo, on drums (who also played in his father Ornette Coleman's group Prime Time). Cortez's work remained highly political; her 1986 album 'Maintain Control' features the song 'Economic Love Song' with the constant refrain throughout the song 'Military spending, huge profits and death.' In 1991, Cortez founded the Organization of Women Writers of Africa. She lived in Dakar, Senegal and in New York City. She died in 2012.

Playwright and writer Lorraine Hansberry was the first African-American author to have a play performed on Broadway. Her best-known work, 'A Raisin in the Sun', is the story of a black family's experiences in south Chicago, and deals with matters of housing, discrimination and racism. The play debuted on Broadway in 1959 with Sidney Poitier, Ruby Dee, Ivan Dixon all in the cast (and Ossie Davis joining later). It was made into a film in 1961.

In New York, Hansberry worked at the Pan-Africanist newspaper 'Freedom' alongside Paul Robeson and W. E. B. Du Bois. She was diagnosed with pancreatic cancer in 1963 and underwent treatment. A year later, Hansberry agreed to speak to winners of a young persons' creative writing conference, where she stated 'Though it is a thrilling and marvelous thing to be merely young and gifted in such times, it is doubly so, doubly dynamic – to be young, gifted and black.' The same year she wrote the text for 'The Movement: Documentary of a Struggle for Equality' about the history of the Student Nonviolent Coordinating Committee (SNCC). Her cancer treatment failed and she died in 1965, aged 34.

Nina Simone co-wrote with Weldon Irvine the song 'To Be Young, Gifted and Black' inspired by her friend Hansberry. Hansberry's ex-husband, Robert Nemiroff, later adapted many of her writings into the play 'To Be Young, Gifted and Black'. A production of this, featuring, among others, the singer and actress Camille Yarborough and James Earl Jones in the cast, was released by the spoken word label, Caedmon Records, in 1971.

DANE BELANY Motivations **Sahara Records** 1975

LORRAINE HANSBERRY To Be Young Gifted And Black **Caedmon Records** 1971
Design by Oration Brooks-El **Photography by** David Attie

ED ROBINSON Black Rhapsody **Human Development Assoc.** 1970
Cover Artwork by Lisa Werchow

ANGELA SIMPSON Angela **Spectrum Records** 1973
Design by James Martin Stulberger

JAYNE CORTEZ Unsubmissive Blues **Bola Press** 1980
Cover Illustration & Photography by Mel Edwards

LANGSTON HUGHES & MARGARET DANNER Writers Of The Revolution **Black Forum** 1970
Photography by Roy DeCarava

Poet and political activist Nikki Giovanni became a key figure in the Black Arts Movement. Her first book 'Black Feeling, Black Talk' (1968), sold more than 10,000 copies in its first year. She founded Niktom, a publishing company, in 1970, commenting 'For $100 you could get 100 books which meant you could sell them at a dollar a book to break even.'

The same year she released her first album 'Truth is on Its Way' with Giovanni voicing her poetry accompanied by the gospel group The New York Community Choir. The record came out through Right-On Records, a small independent New York label. Three years later she released 'Like A Ripple on A Pond' after creating her own record label which she also named Niktom. In 1973, she co-wrote the book 'A Dialogue' with James Baldwin. Giovanni died in 2024.

In April 1968, after the assassination of Martin Luther King Jr., Elaine Brown attended her first meeting of the Los Angeles chapter of the Black Panther Party. She would go on to be the first and only woman to lead the Black Panther Party. Brown was also a singer and released two albums of politically charged songs, 'Seize the Time – The Black Panther Party' (1969) and 'Elaine Brown' (1973), both commissioned by the Party. These albums were arranged and produced by Horace Tapscott, who rehearsed in the same building as the Black Panthers' offices. From 1974 to 1977, Brown chaired the Black Panther Party. She left shortly afterwards, but remains a social activist to this day.

Baltimore-born and raised poet and writer Wanda Robinson released two albums of her poetry on Perception Records, 'Black Ivory' (1971) and 'Me and A Friend' (1973). In fact Robinson was more interested in publishing books and quit the music business after her debut album. 'Me and A Friend' was put together subsequently from extra tracks recorded for 'Black Ivory', with music by Julius Brockington and his band.

Shortly after Robinson changed her name to Laini Mataka. In 1977, she self-published 'Black Rhythms for Fancy Dancers'. Other books published by Black Classic Press include 'Never as Strangers', 'Restoring the Queen', and 'Being a Strong Black Woman Can Getchu Killed'. Poet, writer and publisher Haki R. Madhubuti described Mataka's work as 'a complete repertory of one woman's travels through Black America'. Mataka is today a writer, teacher, and community leader and her most recent book is 'Return of the Kings'.

The Last Poets- were a poetry collective and musical group that arose in the late 1960s, as part of the wave of artists influenced by the Civil Rights Movement and Black nationalism. Their social poetry was accompanied by funk, jazz and Afro-centric percussion (which they labelled 'jazzoetry'). It was ground-breaking, paving the way, along with artists such as Gil Scott-Heron, Sarah Webster Fabio, Nikki Giovanni and other progressive poets, for the arrival of socially-conscious hip-hop in years to come.

The group came out of the East Wind arts workshop in Harlem, a space for theatre, poetry, education and live music. Some of the musicians who played there included Albert Ayler , Pharoah Sanders, Leon Thomas, Lonnie Liston Smith and Sun Ra. In the building next door master drummer Olatunji ran the African Drum and Dance Studio. The group's first album 'The Last Poets' was released in

WANDA ROBINSON Black Ivory **Perception Records** 1971
Photography by Reginald Wickham **Design** James Martin Stulberger

MARTHA JEAN 'THE QUEEN' Just Telling The Truth **Jewel Records 1972**

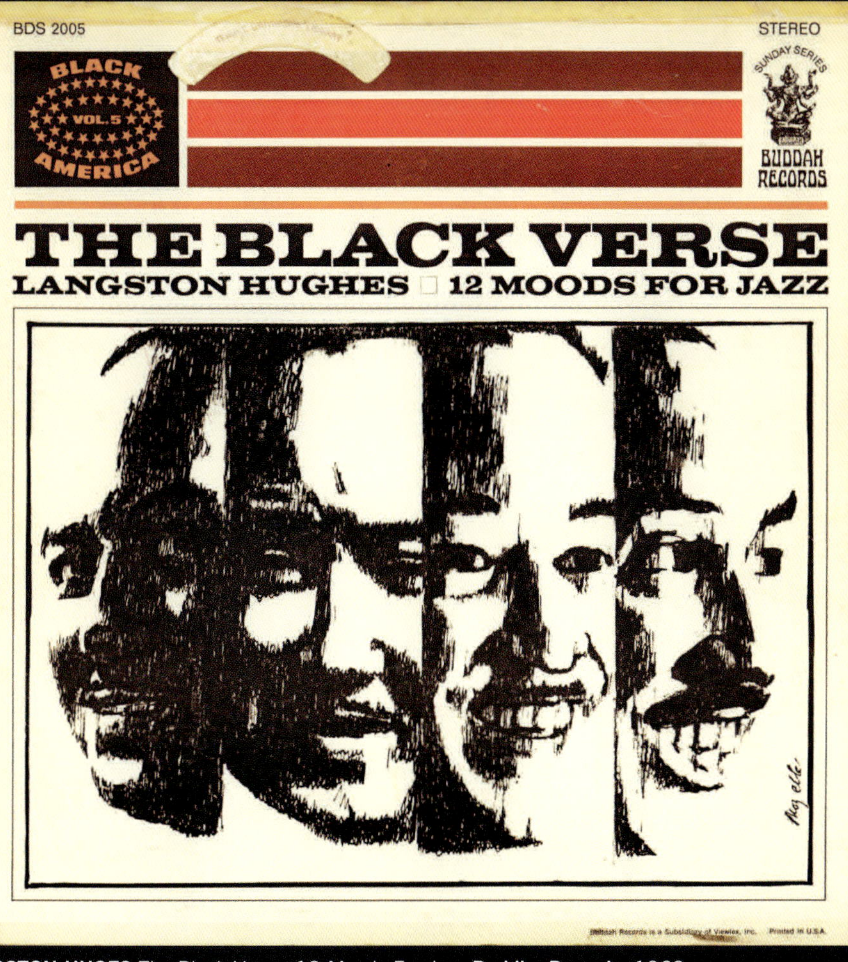

LANGSTON HUGES The Black Verse: 12 Moods For Jazz **Buddha Records** 1969
Artwork by Mozelle Thompson

DICK GREGORY The Light Side: The Dark Side **Poppy Records** 1969
Design by Milton Glaser **Photography by** Elbert Budin

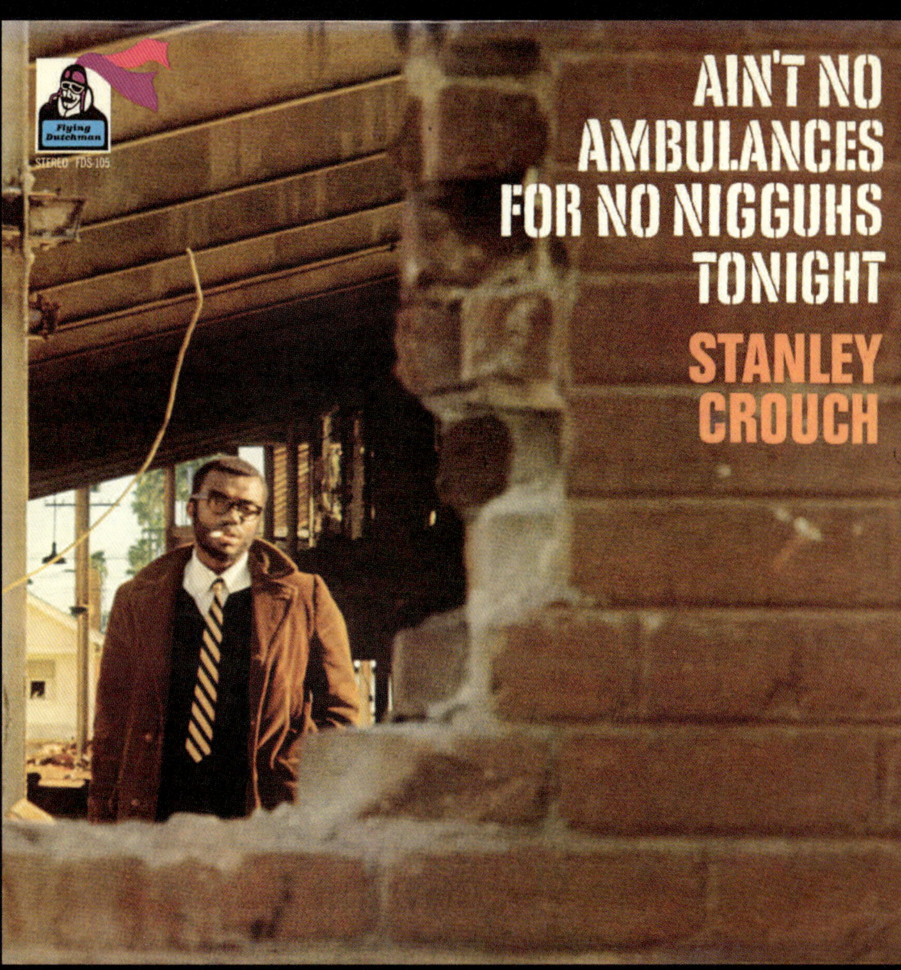

STANLEY CROUCH Ain't No Ambulances For No Nigguhs Tonight **Flying Dutchman** 1969
Design by Robert Flynn **Photography by** Tylon Bareg

MAYA ANGELOU The Poetry Of **Perception Records** 1972
(Originally issued on GWP Records, 1969) **Photography by** Henry Monroe

1970, the first of many in their extensive career. Gylan Kain, an original member of the group, who left before 'The Last Poets' came out, released an album 'The Blue Guerilla' on Juggy Murray's Juggernaut label the same year. In 1972, Imamu Amiri Baraka introduced the group at the Black Spirits Festival of new Black Poets in America, an event captured on record and released on Motown's subsidiary label Black Forum.

West Coast contemporaries of the Last Poets, The Watts Prophets were a similar poetry and music group who formed in 1967, who came out of the Budd Schulberg Watts Writers Workshop, a creative writers group that was created in the wake of the 1965 Watts Riots in South Central Los Angeles. Other writers in the workshop included Quincy Troupe and Wanda Coleman. There was also a theatre component to the workshop, one of whose founders was the actor Yaphet Kotto. The Watts Prophets released two albums, 'The Black Voices On The Streets in Watts' (1970) and 'Rappin' Black in a White World' (1970). This was the first release to use of the term 'Rappin' on an album. Despite little commercial success, the arrival of hip-hop gave their career an extended longevity and the group continue to perform.

Before Maya Angelou became a writer, she trained and performed as a dancer, first in a partnership with choreographer Alvin Ailey, later as a solo dancer. By 1954, she was a professional calypso performer, adopting the name Maya Angelou in place of Marguerite Johnson. In 1957, as a calypso singer she recorded an album 'Miss Calypso', but her main ambition was to be a writer.

In 1959, she moved to New York and

the guidance of her friend James Baldwin, she began work on the book that would become 'I Know Why the Caged Bird Sings'. After meeting Martin Luther King, she organised a Cabaret for Freedom benefit for the Southern Christian Leadership Conference (SCLC) in 1960. Living in Ghana in the early 1960s she met Malcolm X. She returned to the US in 1965, planning to build a new civil rights group 'The Organization of Afro-American Unity' with X, but he was assassinated shortly after her return. 'I Know Why the Caged Bird', her first book, was published in 1969. The same year GWP, a small New York record label, released 'The Poetry of Maya Angelou', an album of Angelou reciting some of her poems, including 'No No No No', 'Letter to an Aspiring Junkie', 'Harlem Hopscotch', 'Re: Revolt,' 'Black Ode' and more with liner notes by James Baldwin.

The selection of spoken word albums featured here shows how powerfully the Black Arts Movement successfully brought together manifold forms of performative expression into a collective voice, whether it be the biting humour of comedian, social critic and activist Dick Gregory, or the sermon-like thoughts of Martha Jean 'The Queen' Steinberg, ordained minister and one of the earliest female radio R&B, gospel and social commentary DJs in the United States.

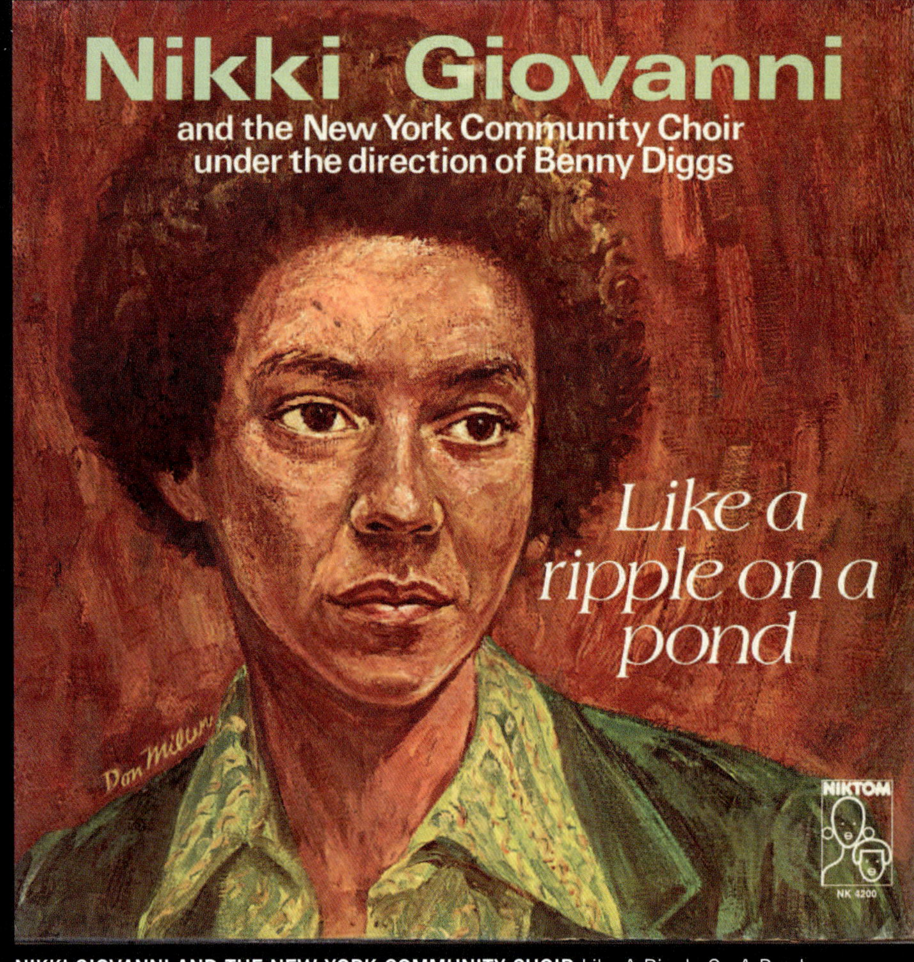

NIKKI GIOVANNI AND THE NEW YORK COMMUNITY CHOIR Like A Ripple On A Pond **Niktom** 1973 **Cover design and portrait by** Don Miller

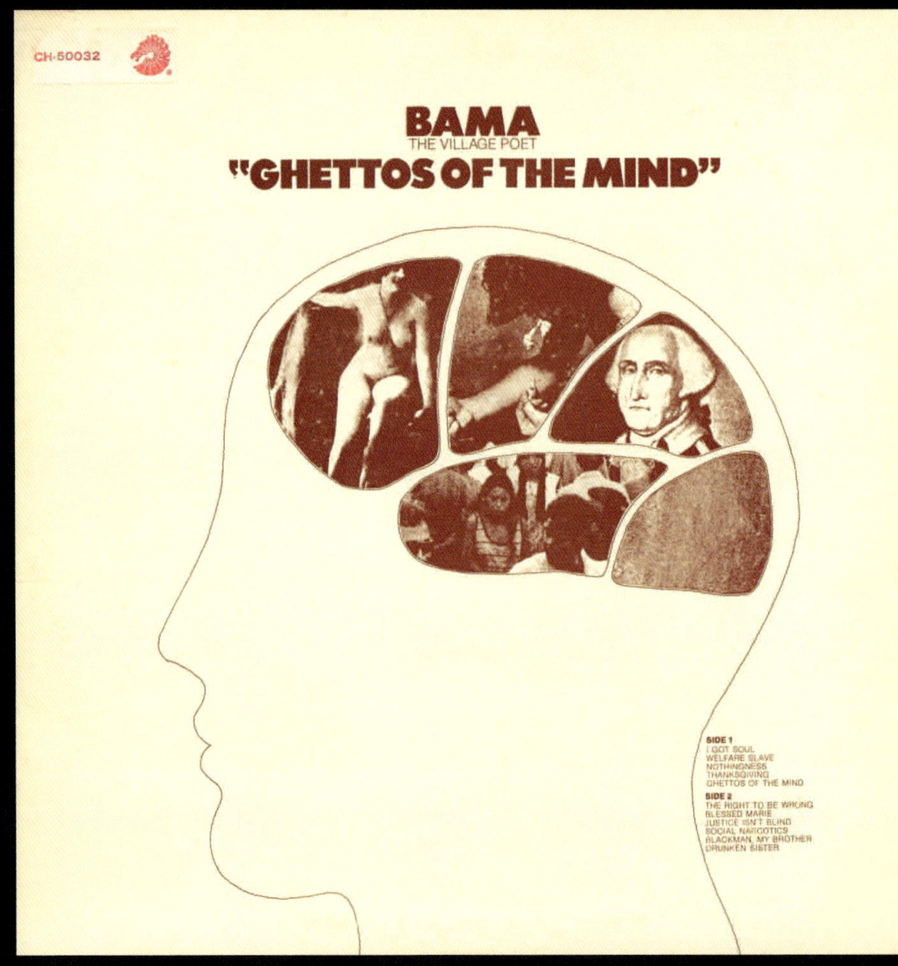

BAMA - THE VILLAGE POET Ghettos Of The Mind **Chess** 1972

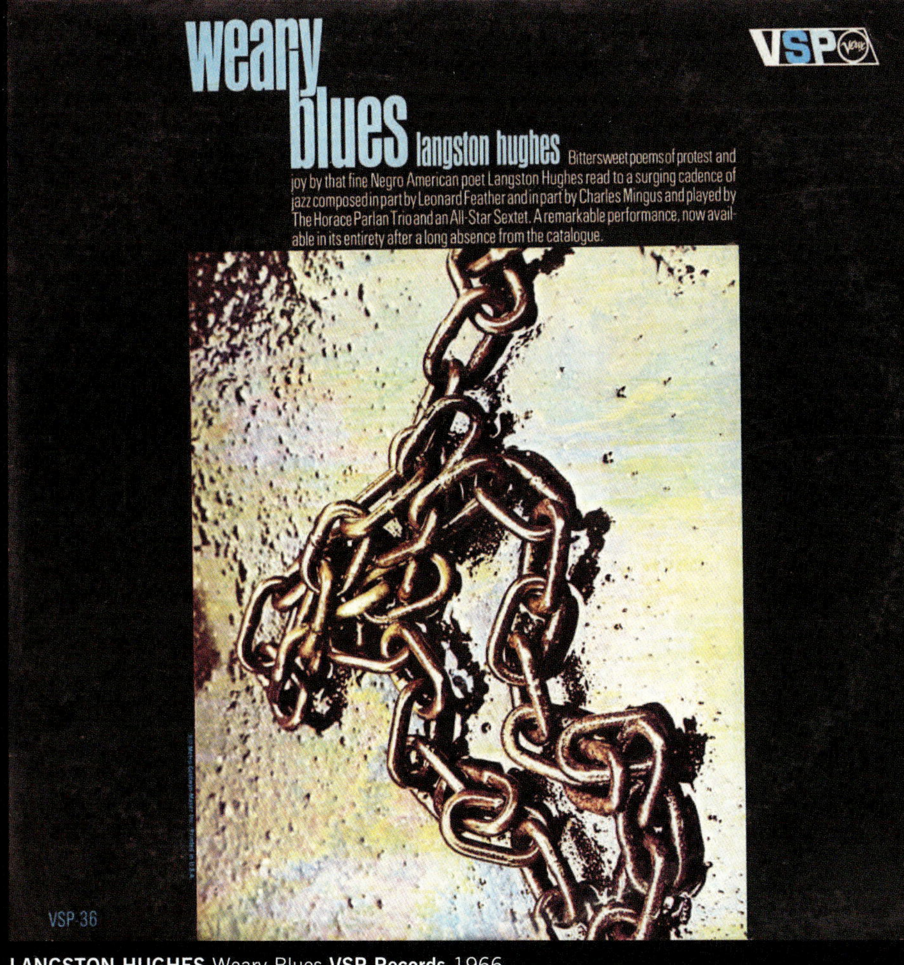

LANGSTON HUGHES Weary Blues **VSP Records** 1966
Cover by Fran Scott **Photography by** Roy De Carava

JAYNE CORTEZ & THE FIRESPITTERS Maintain Control **Bola Press** 1986
Illustration by Mel Edwards

WANDA ROBINSON Me And A Friend Perception Records 1973
Photography by Reginald Wickham **Album Design** James Martin Stulberger

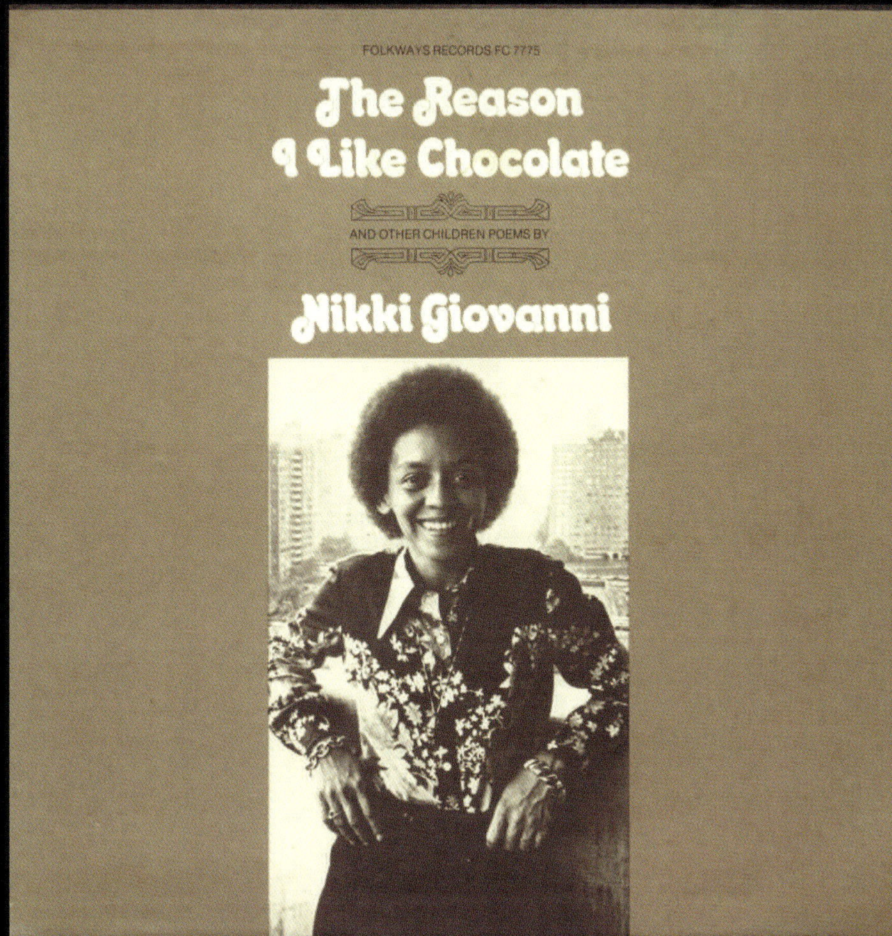

NIKKI GIOVANNI The Reason I Like Chocolate

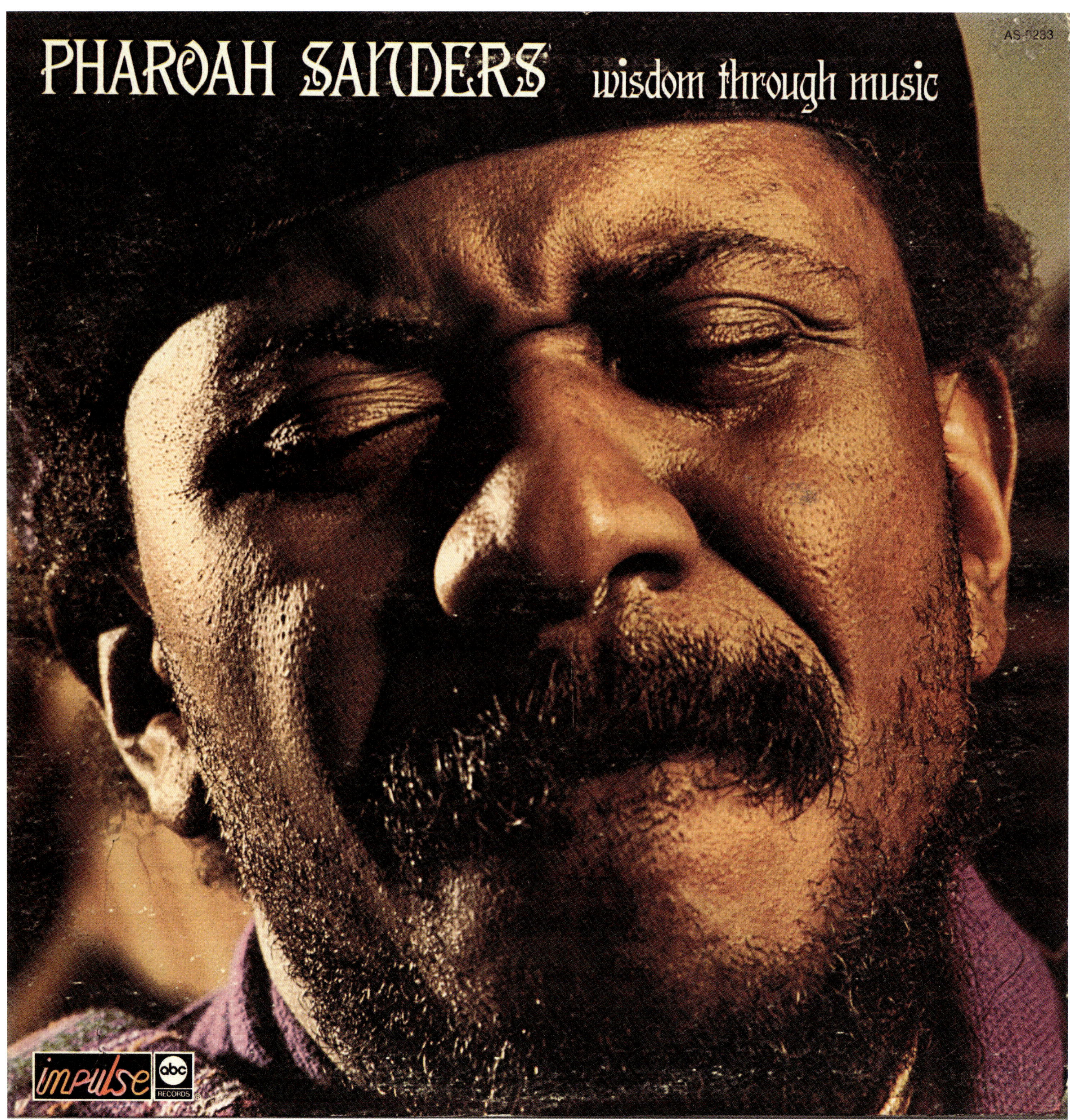

PHAROAH SANDERS Wisdom Through Music **Impulse** 1973
Cover Artwork by Alan Sekuler **Photography by** Chuck Stewart

MARZETTE WATTS Marzette And Company **ESP-Disk'** 1968
Photography by James Maninis

JULIUS HEMPHILL Dogon A.D. **Mbari** 1972

30 AM 6111

jacques coursil

« black suite »

JACQUES COURSIL Black Suite **America Records** 1971 (originally released on BYG Records 1971)
Photography by Jacques Bisceglia, Nadja Pictures

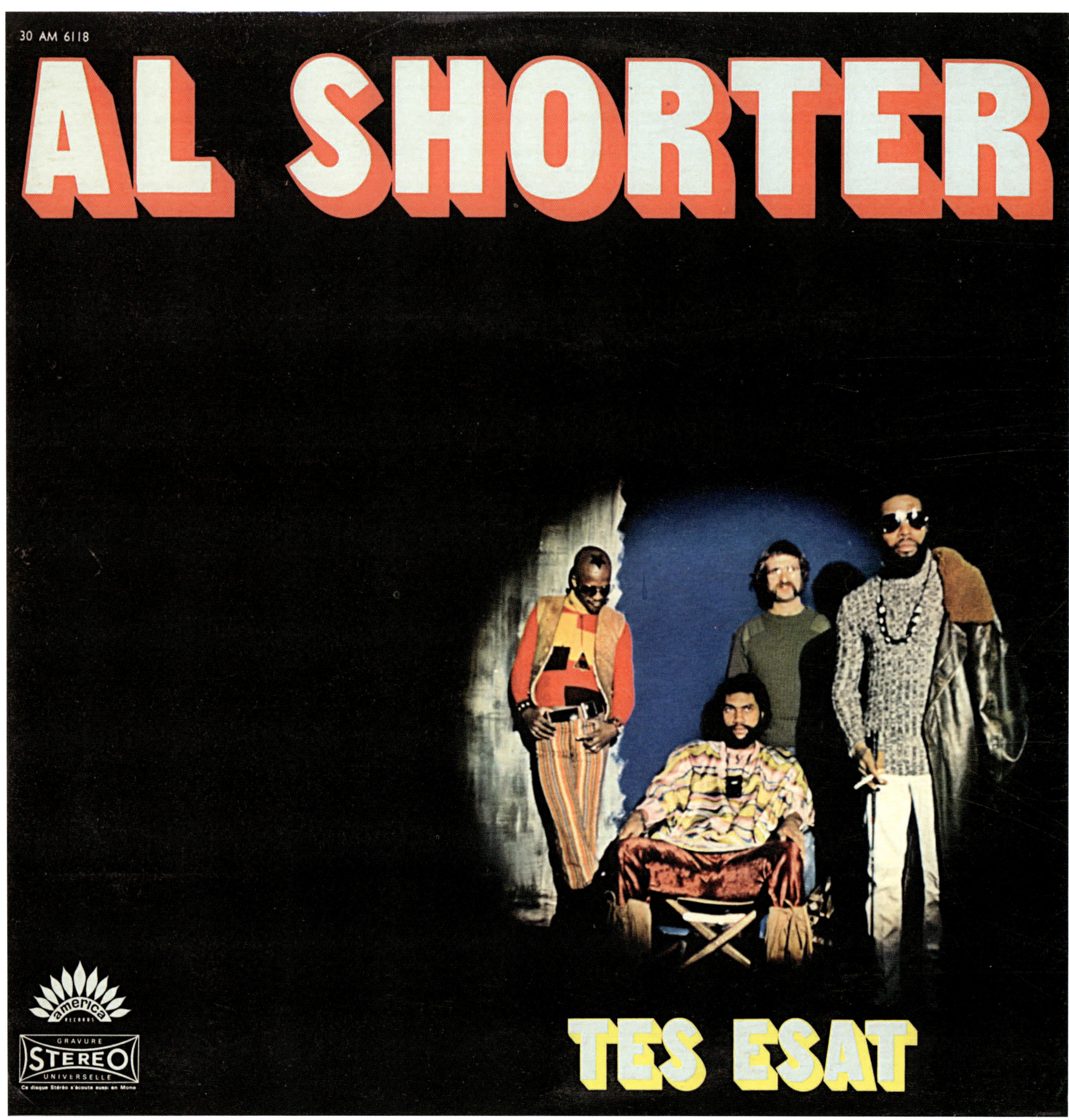

AL SHORTER Tes Esat **America Records** 1971
Photography by Gilbert Moreau

CONRAD BENJAMIN Saturn **Nebula** 1982
Design by Jack Ellison **Photography by** Bob Stewart

HORACE TAPSCOTT Songs Of The Unsung **Interplay Records** 1978
Photography by Bill Dow

IMANI Out Of The Blue **Self Released** 1983
Artwork by James McCabe

M'BOOM Re: Percussion **Strata East Records** 1973

GEORGE RUSSELL Electronic Sonata For Souls Loved by Nature **Strata-East Records** 1976 (Originally issued on Flying Dutchman, 1971) **Artwork by** Anna Russell **Photography** Barry Savenor

FAMOUDOU DON MOYE - ARI BROWN Live At The Progressive Arts Center **L'Orsa Maggiore** 1982 **Cover Artwork by** Mauizio Carioli **Photography by** Elena Carminati

ANDREW CYRILLE & MAONO Metamusicians' Stomp **Black Saint** 1978 **Artwork and Photography by** Giuseppe Pino **Design by** Gigi Barbieri

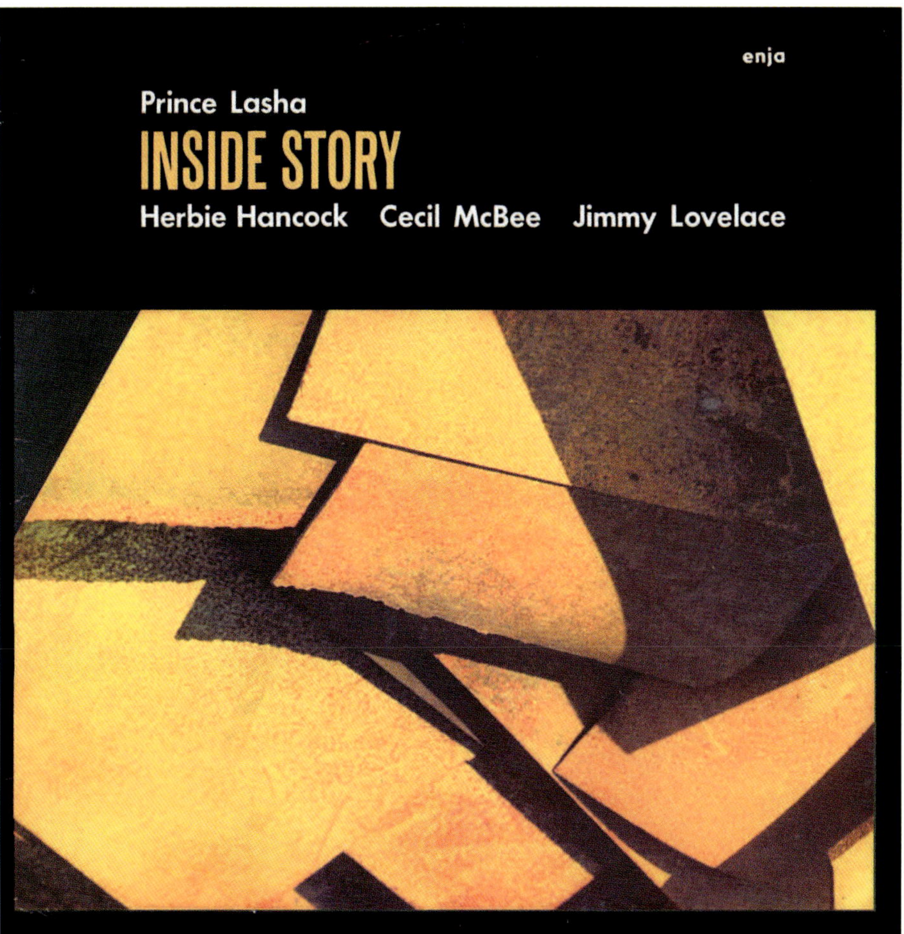

PRINCE LASHA Inside Story **Enja Records** 1981 (but recorded in 1965) **Photography by** Franz Hofer

AIR Air Song **India Navigation** 1982 (Originally issued on Whynot, Japan, 1975)
Photography by Masahiko Yuh

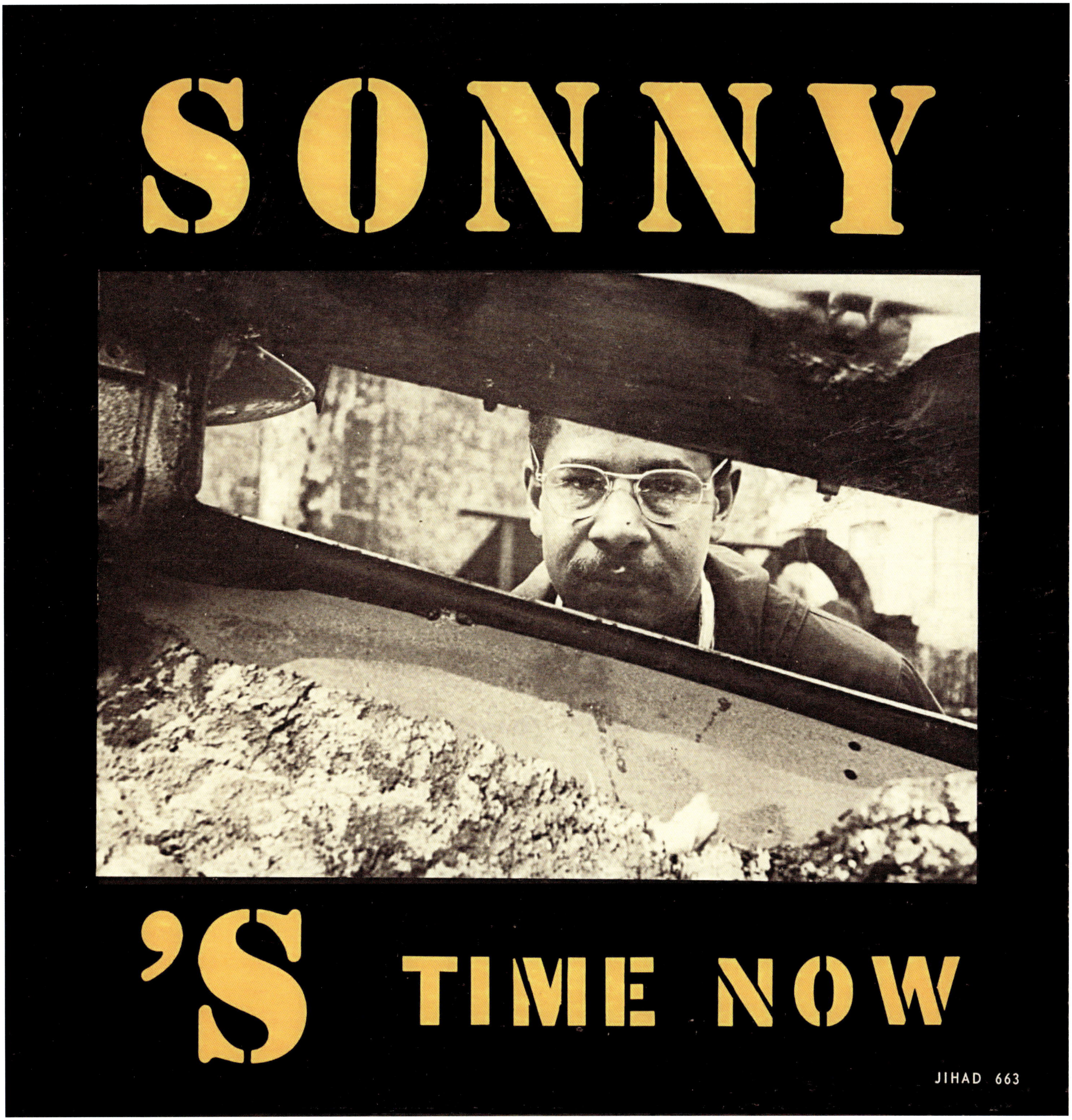

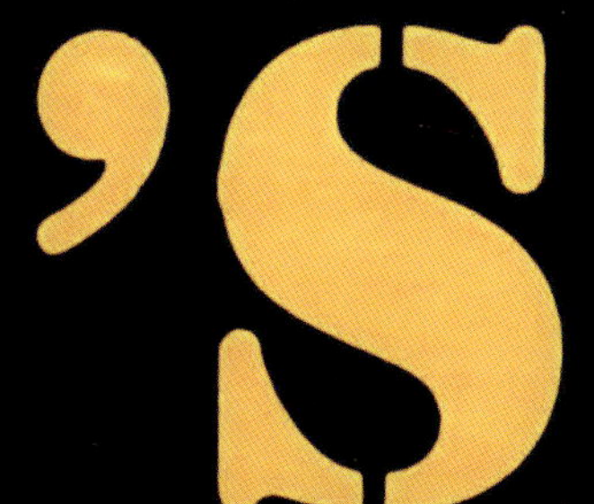

SONNY MURRAY Sonny's Time Now **Jihad Productions** 1965

MALAKU DAKU FEATURING THE BUMP BANG U BANG Love Drums From The Ghetto **Chaka Unlimited** 1974

JO GRINAGE Mother's Love Song **Dakeeta Records** 1971
Design by Cecil Elombe Brath **Photography by** Ronnie Brathwaite

MAL WALDRON All Alone **Globe Records** 1969 (Originally released on GTA Records, Italy, 1966)
Design by Paolo Piccolo **Photography by** Mario Orfini

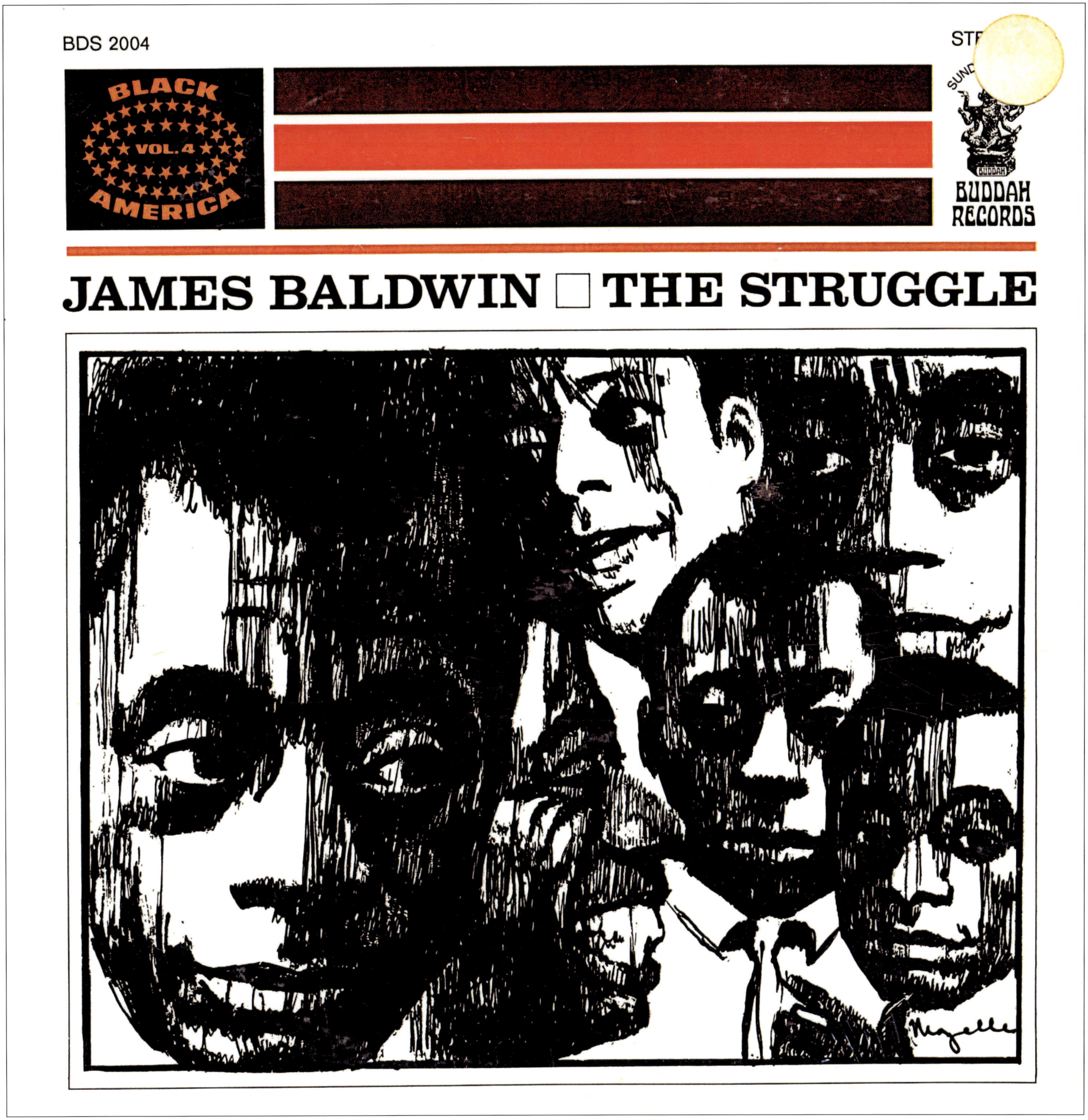

BDS 2004

JAMES BALDWIN □ THE STRUGGLE

JAMES BALDWIN The Struggle **Buddah Records** 1969
Cover Artwork by Mozelle Thompson

ROSCOE MITCHELL Old / Quartet **Nessa Records** 1975
Graphics by Tannenbaum Design

LESTER BOWIE Rope-A-Dope **Muse Records** 1976
Art Direction, Graphics and Photography by Hal Wilson

CLEVELAND EATON AND THE KATS Half and Half Volume 1 **Cle An Thair Records** 1972
Cover Artwork by C. Eaton II

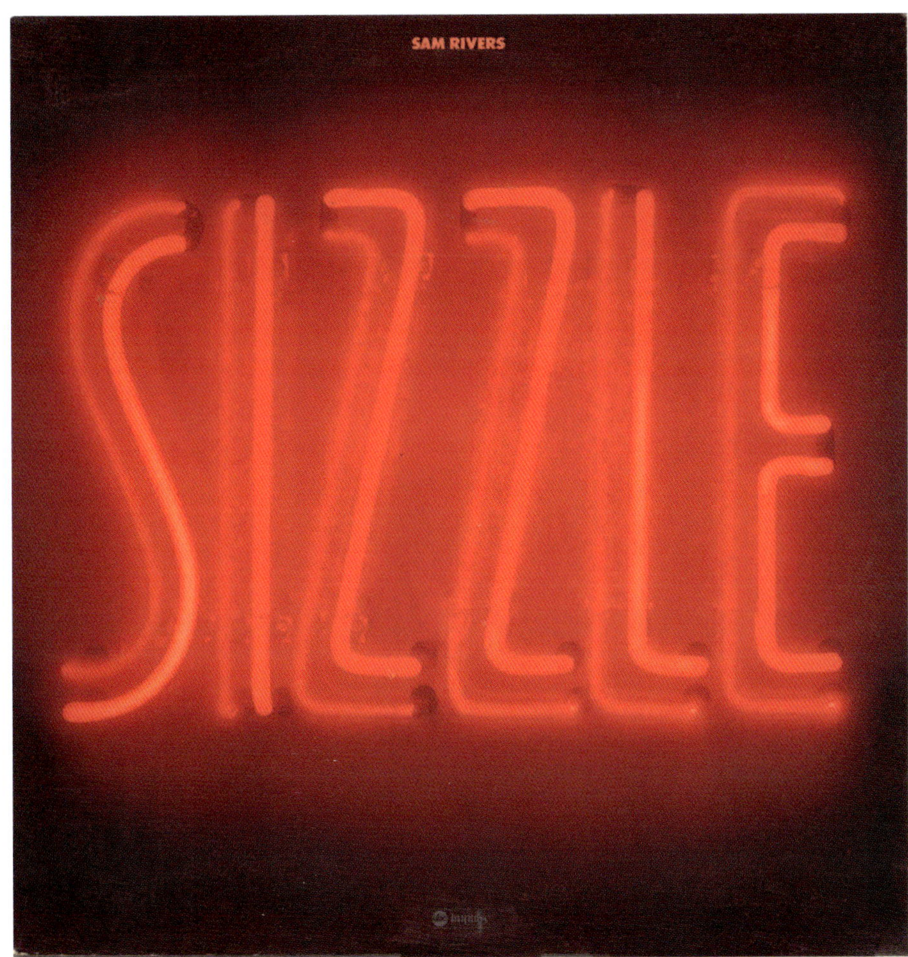

SAM RIVERS Sizzle **ABC Impulse!** 1976
Art Direction by Tom Wilkes **Design by** Martin Donald

ANTHONY DAVIS QUARTET Song For The Old World **India Navigation** 1978
Cover Artwork by Nanette Gianantoni **Photography by** Karen Clemens

NATHAN DAVIS Happy Girl **SABA** 1965
Graphics by Gigi Berendt **Photography by** Manfred Schaeffer

The unique voice of th
JEANNE LEE with
RAN BLAKE at the piano

THE NEWEST SOUND AROUND

"HIS MASTER'S VOICE"
RCA VICTOR

If there's going to be an enduring "new wave" in jazz styling . . . this voice, this piano may well be the beginning.

Laura · Blue Monk · Church on Russell Street · Where Flamingos Fly · Season in the Sun · Summertime · Lover Man · Evil Blues · Sometimes I Feel Like a Motherless Child · When Sunny Gets Blue · Love Isn't Everything

LPM-2500

JEANNE LEE & RAN BLAKE The Newest Sound Around **RCA** 1962

CIVIL RIGHTS AND BLACK POWER SPEECHES

Martin Luther King's most famous 'I Have A Dream' speech was delivered on August 28, 1963, during the March on Washington for Jobs and Freedom. King had also given a precursor to this speech at the Cobo Hall, Detroit, June 23, 1963 at the Detroit 'Freedom Rally' in front of an estimated 125,000 people, at the time one of the largest civil rights demonstrations.

The event was captured by Motown Records who released an album of the speech the same year, produced by Berry Gordy himself. Motown was a rising force in popular music and King's album underscored the label's connection to the Civil Rights Movement.

Five years later, the label released the album 'Free at Last' which includes 'I've Been To The Mountain Top' delivered in Memphis, Tennessee, on April 3, 1968 the evening before Martin Luther King's assassination. 'Free at Last' was the first of over a dozen recordings of King's speeches posthumously released that year.

In 1970, Motown created the Black Forum subsidiary which issued important and polemical recordings by Martin Luther King, Stokely Carmichael, Langston Hughes, Amiri Baraka and Ossie Davis. Black Forum also released an album by Elaine Brown, the only female leader of the Black Panthers, which was produced by Fonce Mizell and arranged by Horace Tapscott.

Flying Dutchman Records, aside from Leon Thomas, Gil-Scott Heron, Lonnie Liston Smith and other jazz artists, also released a number of highly-charged political albums documenting some key figures in the Black Power Movement. These included H Rap Brown, the Black Panther Party's minister of justice; feminist, communist, academic and Black Panther Angela Davis; cultural critic , writer and musician Stanley Crouch's 'Ain't No Ambulances For No Nigguhs Tonight'; and a series of polemical texts by Peter Hammill, voiced by radio DJ William Roscoe Mercer, aka Rosko including 'Massacre at My Lai' and 'Murder at Kent State University'. 'A Night at Santa Rita', by Ramparts magazine editor Robert Scheers was his account of the brutal incarceration of protesters after a Berkeley 1969 People's Park demonstration also voiced by Rosco, with accompanying music scored by Ron Carter and James Spaulding.

Civil rights activist and Baptist minister Rev. Jesse Jackson's 'I Am Somebody' was released on Respect records in 1971. Jackson recites a poem by Reverend William Holmes Borders, also a minister and civil rights leader, written in the 1950s

I am Somebody! I am Somebody!
I may be poor, But I am Somebody.
I may be young, But I am Somebody.
I may be on welfare, But I am Somebody.
I may be small, But I am Somebody.
I may have made mistakes, But I am Somebody.
My clothes are different, My face is different,
My hair is different, But I am Somebody.
I am Black, Brown, or white.

LP 1300

The Last Message

Malcolm X

MALCOLM X The Last Message **All Platinum** 1973

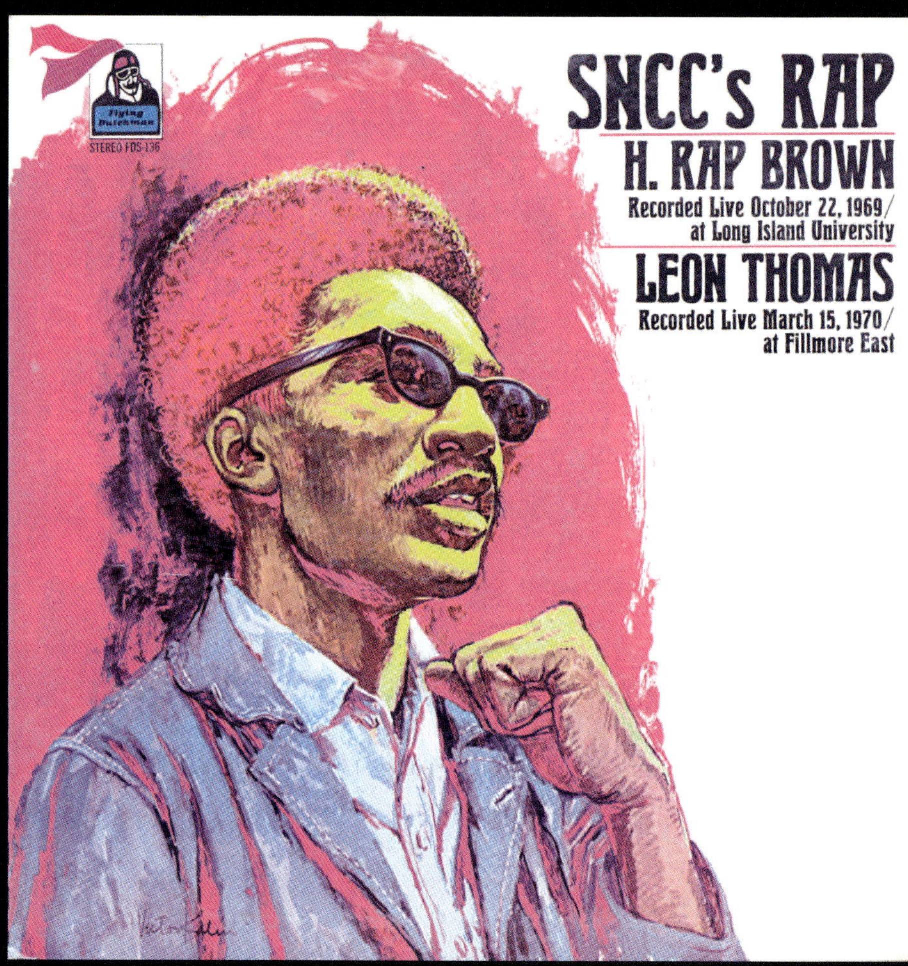

H. RAP BROWN / LEON THOMAS SNCC's Rap **Flying Dutchman** 1970
Illustration by Victor Kalin

DR MARTIN LUTHER KING JR Message To The World… It's Midnight **UpFront Records** 1968
Design by Lee-Myles Assoc.

ANGELA DAVIS Soul and Soledad **Flying Dutchman** 1971

ELDRIDGE CLEAVER Soul On Wax **More Record Company** 1968
Design by Milton Tuitt **Photography by** Howard Stein

DR MARTIN LUTHER KING JR A Knock At Midnight **Creed Records** 1968
Cover Artwork by Dan Quest Art Studio

I speak a different language
But I must be respected, Protected,
Never rejected. I am God's child!

Jackson reprised the poem on many occasions including an appearance on Sesame Street in 1971, and in his introduction to the Watt Stax music festival in 1972. The JB's used the poem on the track 'Same Beat' which appeared on their 1974 album 'Damn Right I Am Somebody.'

Eldridge Cleaver was an early leader of the Black Panthers, and at various points Minister of Information and Head of the International Section of the Panthers. In the aftermath of the assassination of Martin Luther King Jr. on April 4, 1968, riots took place across America. Oakland police officers confronted a group of Black Panthers including Cleaver; a shootout ensued and two officers were wounded and Black Panther Bobby Hutton died. Facing charges of murder Cleaver later fled the USA to avoid arrest, first to Cuba, then to Algeria where he attended the Pan-African Cultural festival in 1969, as did other Black Panther members and a number of African-American writers and jazz musicians including Maya Angelou, Nina Simone, Haki R. Madhubuti and Archie Shepp. Shepp performed with a group of Algerian and Tuareg drummers as well as with Sunny Murray, Clifford Thornton and Grachan Moncur (an album of this concert was released by BYG/Actuel in 1971).

'Soul on Ice', Cleaver's collection of essays written while he had earlier served time in prison in San Quentin and Folsom State Prison, a searing indictment on white society and the black experience, was published in 1968. The same year an album, 'Eldridge Cleaver Recorded at Syracuse' recorded on Jul 28, 1968 (recorded four months after the shootout) was released by the More Record Company. This album was re-released two years later as 'Soul on Wax', capitalising on the notoriety of 'Soul on Ice.'

There are around a dozen recordings of Malcolm X but Malcolm X's 'Speaking', released on Ethnic Records in 1965, was the only one to come out while he was still alive. It was later reissued by Harlem record producer Paul Winley. Winley had started his career releasing doo-wop on his Paul Winley Records label in the 1950s. After doo wop fell out of fashion, Winley resurfaced as an early exponent of hip-hop releasing early rap records by his daughters Paulette and Tanya Winley, and Afrika Bambaataa. Aware of the interest in Malcolm X to young rap fans to sample, Winley issued a number of his speeches including 'Speaking' under the title 'The Ballot or The Bullet'.

'The Last Message' was issued on All Platinum Records, owned by Sylvia and Joe Robinson, two figures who would also prove to be highly significant figures in hip-hop when they created Sugarhill Records in 1979.

Malcolm X's 'The Last Message' ends with the following words: 'I say again that I am not a racist, I don't believe in any form of segregation or anything like that. I am for the brotherhood of everybody, but I don't believe in forcing brotherhood upon people who don't want it. As long as we practice brotherhood among ourselves, and then others who want to practice brotherhood with us, we practice it with them also, we're for that. But I don't think that we should run around trying to love somebody who doesn't love us.'

THE AFRO-AMERICAN'S QUEST FOR EDUCATION A Black Odyssey - Adventures In Negro History Volume III **Pepsi Cola Records** 1969

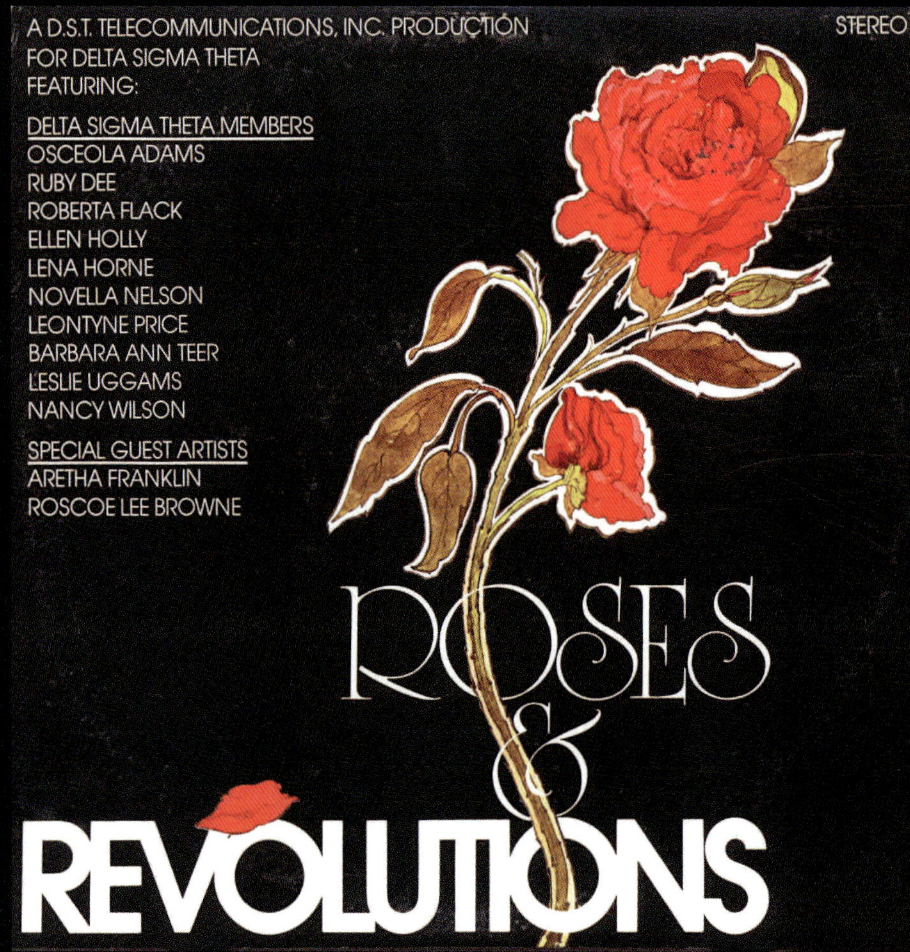

VARIOUS ARTISTS Roses and Revolutions **D.S.T. Telecommunications Inc.** 1975
Design by Melody Corbett and Tony Paris

ONLY AUTHORIZED VERSION

...free at last

DR. MARTIN LUTHER KING, JR.

Mountaintop

I Have a Dream

Drum Major Instinct

929

DR MARTIN LUTHER KING JR Free At Last **Gordy Records** 1968
Design by Herbart

REVEREND JESSE JACKSON I Am Somebody **Respect** 1971

THE GREAT ONES: Famous American Negroes and Their Achievements
Westinghouse Broadcast Company 1967

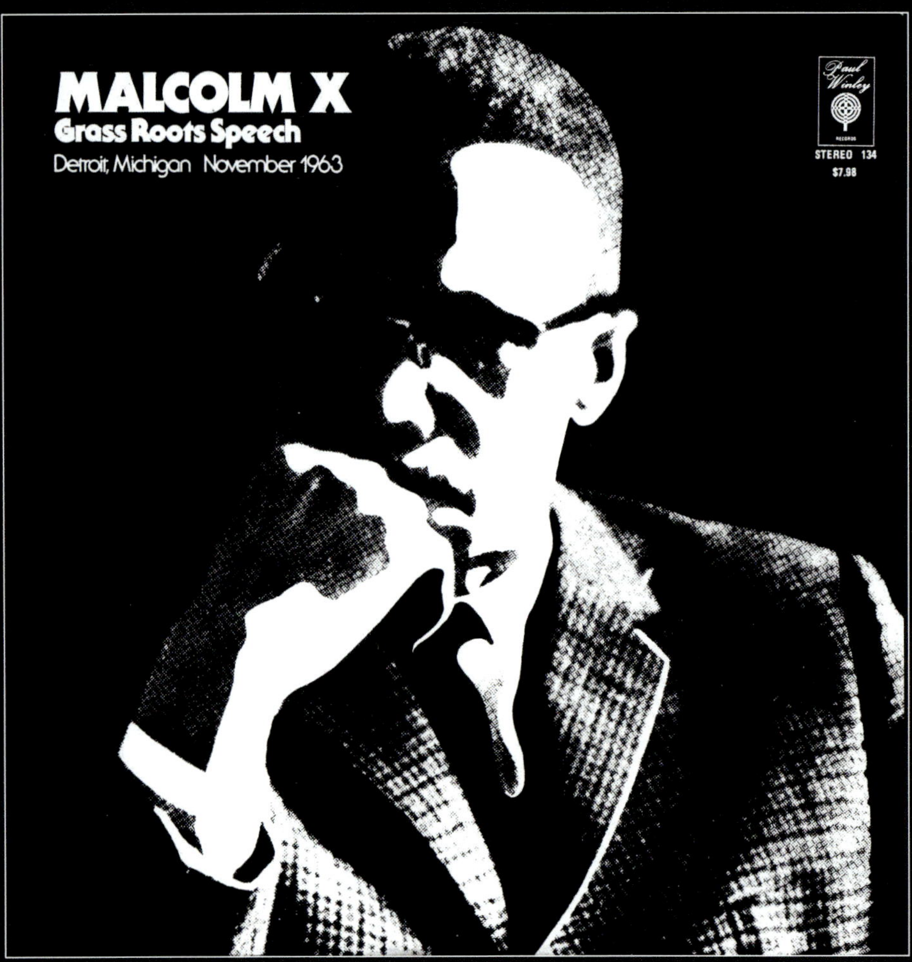

MALCOLM X Grass Roots Speech Detroit, Michigan November 1963 **Paul Winley Records** 1979

Adventures in Negro History Volume 1

THE GREAT MARCH TO FREEDOM

REV. MARTIN LUTHER KING *Speaks*

DETROIT JUNE 23,1963

REVEREND MARTIN LUTHER KING The Great March To Freedom **Gordy** 1963

THE REVEREND DR. MARTIN LUTHER KING JR I Have a Dream - The Original Address From The March On Washington August 1963 **20th Century Fox Records** 1968

THE JUGGY MURRAY ORCHESTRA I have a dream **Sue Records**

THE REVEREND DR MARTIN LUTHER KING JR In Search of Freedom **Mercury** 1968

RE: RECORDS

STEREO - RE 3117

THE PSYCHE

REVOLUTIONARY ENSEMBLE

REVOLUTIONARY ENSEMBLE The Psyche **Re: Records** 1975

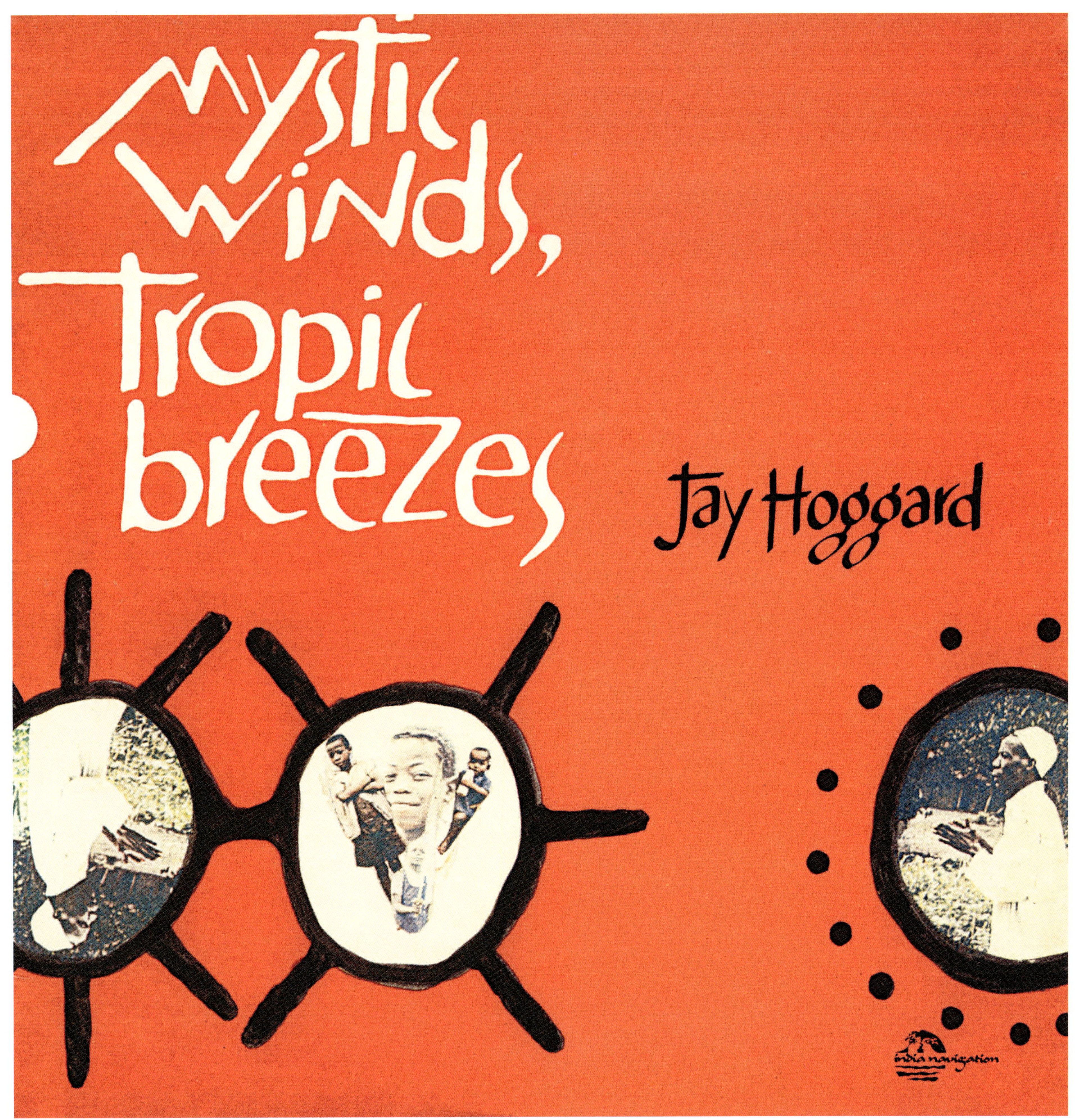

JAY HOGGARD Mystic Winds, Tropic Breezes **India Navigation** 1982
Design by Elsie Tredricks **Illustration by** Wendel White **Photography by** Beth Cummins

JOHN COLTRANE A Love Supreme **Impulse!** 1965
Design by George Gray and Viceroy

A Love Supreme

John Coltrane recorded ‘A Love Supreme’ in one take at Rudy Van Gelder’s studio in Englewood Cliffs, New Jersey on Dec 9, 1964, with his quartet comprised of pianist McCoy Tyner, bassist Jimmy Garrison and Elvin Jones on drums. When the album was released the following January, it was immediately hailed by critics as a masterpiece and became an instant bestseller. Deeply spiritual, highly improvisational and yet also structured, the music defied categorisation. ‘A Love Supreme’ was free jazz, devotional, avant-garde, modal, ‘an epic aural poem to man’s place in God’s plan’.

Creed Taylor brought Coltrane to Impulse! Records in 1961. Bob Thiele was employed as in-house producer and almost immediately began working with Coltrane. Thiele recognised the importance in Coltrane’s music and made it possible for him to record at any opportunity, much to the dismay of his paymasters. Similarly, on the advice of Coltrane, Thiele brought in artists to the label from Coltrane’s circle – Archie Shepp, Pharoah Sanders, McCoy Tyner, Alice Coltrane.

‘A Love Supreme’ was released at the height of Coltrane’s creative powers. By 1964 he was carving out a new pathway for modern jazz. His music was at once radical, angry, political, spiritual, beautiful, profound, complex, intense. Whichever way you looked at it Coltrane had become the true leader of this musical movement.

Still to come, in the two years before Coltrane would pass, were even more boundary-pushing albums including ‘Ascension’ and ‘Meditation’. ‘Expression’ released two months after his death in 1967, became the first in a number of Coltrane albums that Thiele had fortunately been stockpiling.

Aside from the music of ‘A Love Supreme’, perhaps the most radical achievement that Coltrane achieved was to shift the perspective on what jazz music should sound like to the public, the critics and the record industry alike.

‘A Love Supreme’ was ‘outside’ music created on the ‘inside’ of the mainstream music industry. Utterly avant-garde, it is also one of the best-selling jazz records of all time. Coltrane reconciled these apparently contradictory concepts - for ‘A Love Supreme’, there was no distinction between the two. Coltrane subverted the music industry and its values, creating a record totally on his own terms.

Design by Joe Lebow **Painting by** Victor Kalin

SUN RA Super Sonic Sounds **Impulse!** 1974 (Originally issued on El Saturn Records, 1957)
Cover Artwork by Tim Bryant

KAIN The Blue Guerrilla **Juggernaut Records** 1970
Design by PAS Studios **Painting by** Abu. Bakr Abdullah

BLACK JAZZ RECORDS

Black Jazz Records was founded in Oakland, California, by pianist Gene Russell and percussionist Dick Schory. The label released twenty albums between 1971 and 1975. Artists who recorded for Black Jazz Records included Cleveland Eaton (bassist for Ramsey Lewis), keyboardists Doug Carn and Chester Thompson, vocalist Kellee Patterson, saxophonist Rudolph Johnson, bassist Henry Franklin, and spiritual fusion group The Awakening.

The label was distributed and financed by Ovation Records, based in Chicago. Schory founded Ovation in 1969, shortly after leaving RCA. Schory was a Grammy-nominated percussionist who was also known for his development of the stereo recording techniques including Dynagroove, and RCA Victor's Stereo Action. Schory also pioneered quadrophonic sound, and a number of Black Jazz Records were in quadrophonic and other formats such as ¼" tape and 8-track.

Black Jazz launched in 1971 with Gene Russell's 'New Direction'. Russell was the creative force behind the label, acting as producer, engineer and A&R and focussed on developing new solo artists. The most successful of these was Doug Carn, who released four albums featuring his wife, Jean Carn, as vocalist. She later changed her name to Jean Carne and became a successful soul singer signed to Gamble and Huff's Philadelphia International empire.

Singer Kellee Patterson gained notice as the first black Miss Indiana in 1971, before recording Maiden Voyage', her debut album for the label. Keyboardist Chester Thompson would go on to join Tower of Power and later Santana. The Awakening featured top veteran musicians from Chicago - the only Chicago group signed to the label. Drummer and percussionist Arlington Davis Jr, bassist Reggie Willis, flautist and tenor saxophonist Richard (Ari) Brown and trumpeter Frank Gordon were all members of the Association For The Advancement Of Creative Musicians. Trombonist Steve Galloway and Ken Chaney were part of Philip Cohran and The Artistic Ensemble.

Black Jazz Records released 20 or so superlative albums in a four-year period, all successfully blending spiritual jazz, funk and soul jazz. The label closed in 1975.

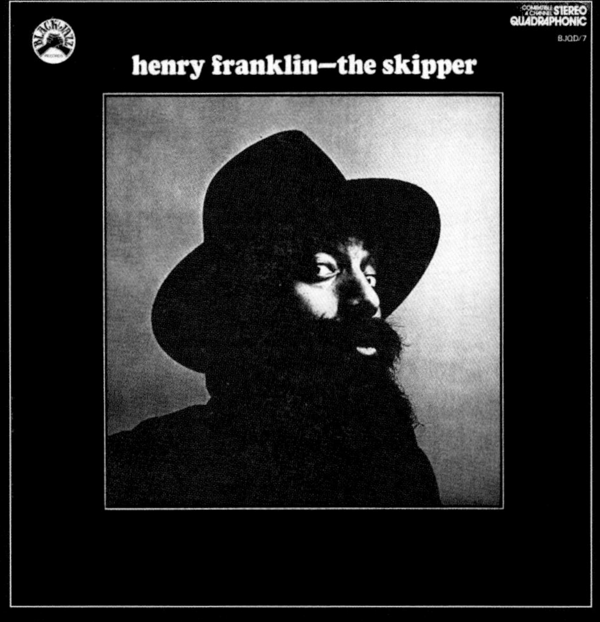

HENRY FRANKLIN The Skipper **Black Jazz Records** 1972 **Design by** Dorothy Tanous **Artwork by** Bud Doty

DOUG CARN FEATURING JEAN CARN Spirit Of The New Land **Black Jazz Records** 1972 **Design by** Dorothy Tanous **Artwork by** Bud Doty

RUDOLPH JOHNSON Spring Rain **Black Jazz Records** 1971 **Cover Artwork & Photography by** Dorothy Tanous **Design by** Ray Lawrence Ltd

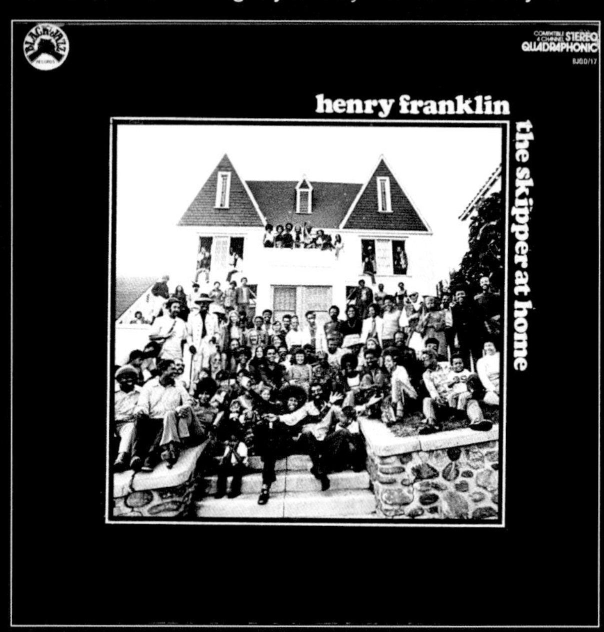

HENRY FRANKLIN The Skipper at Home **Black Jazz Records** 1974 **Photography by** Bruce Wilson

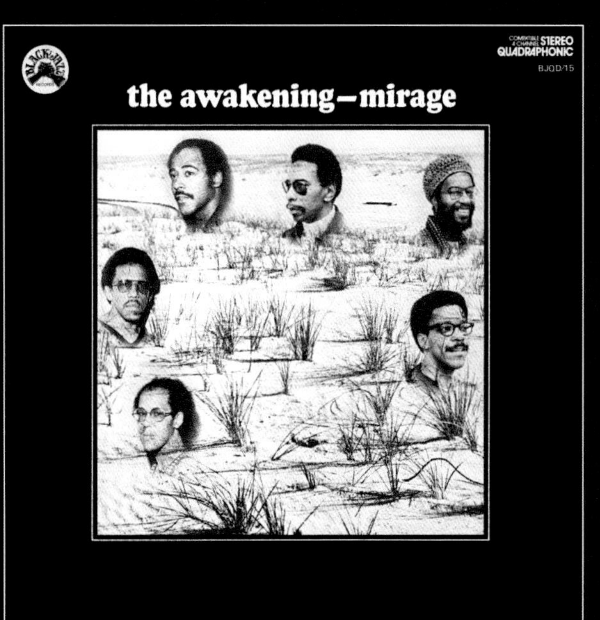

THE AWAKENING Mirage **Black Jazz Records** 1973 **Artwork by** Bud Doty **Photography by** Jerome Presley

DOUG CARN FEATURING JEAN CARN Revelation **Black Jazz Records** 1973 **Photography by** Judson Brown

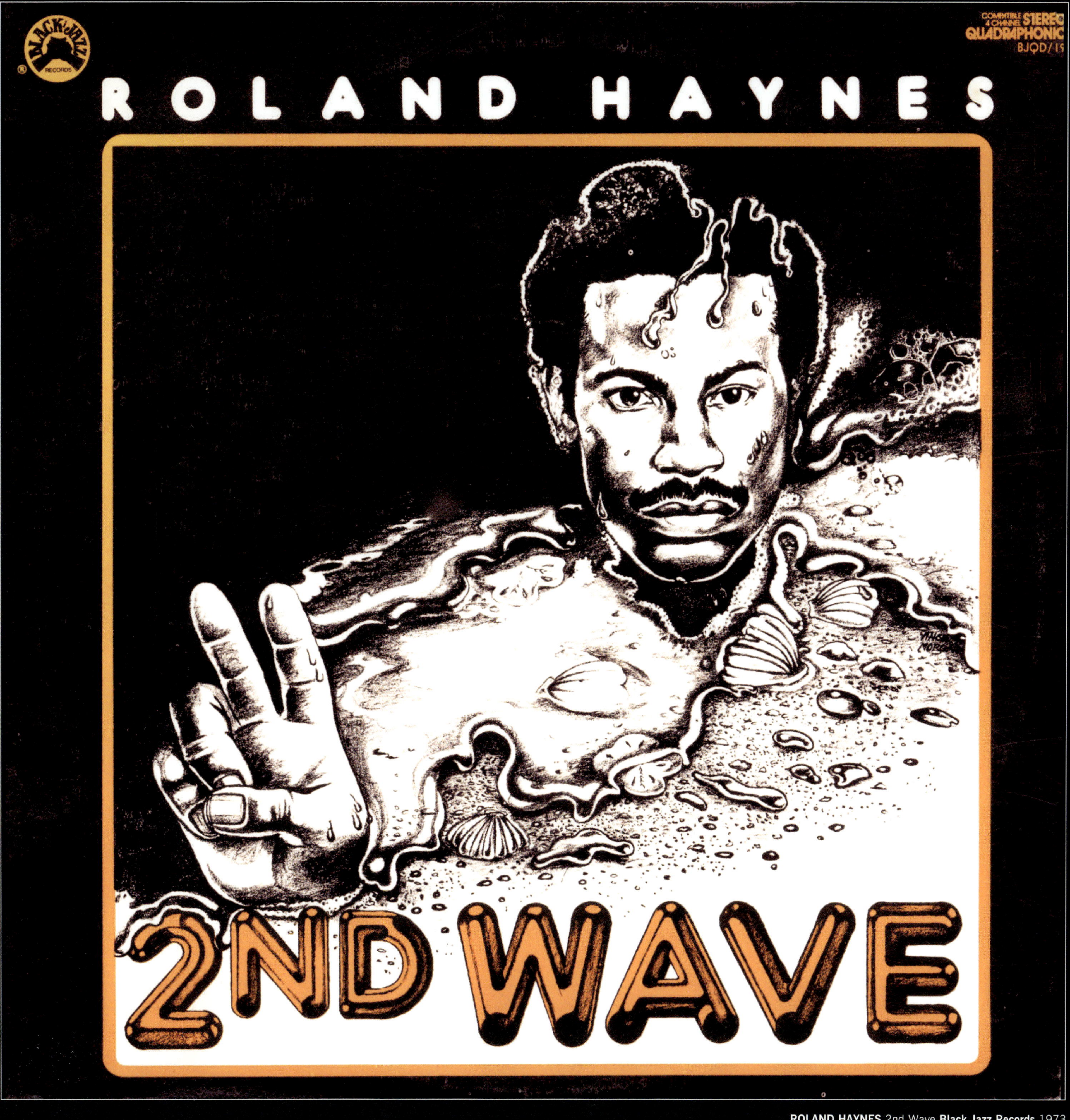

BLACK JAZZ RECORDS

ROLAND HAYNES

2ND WAVE

ROLAND HAYNES 2nd Wave **Black Jazz Records** 1973
Illustration by Vince Morgan **Graphics by** Grafica

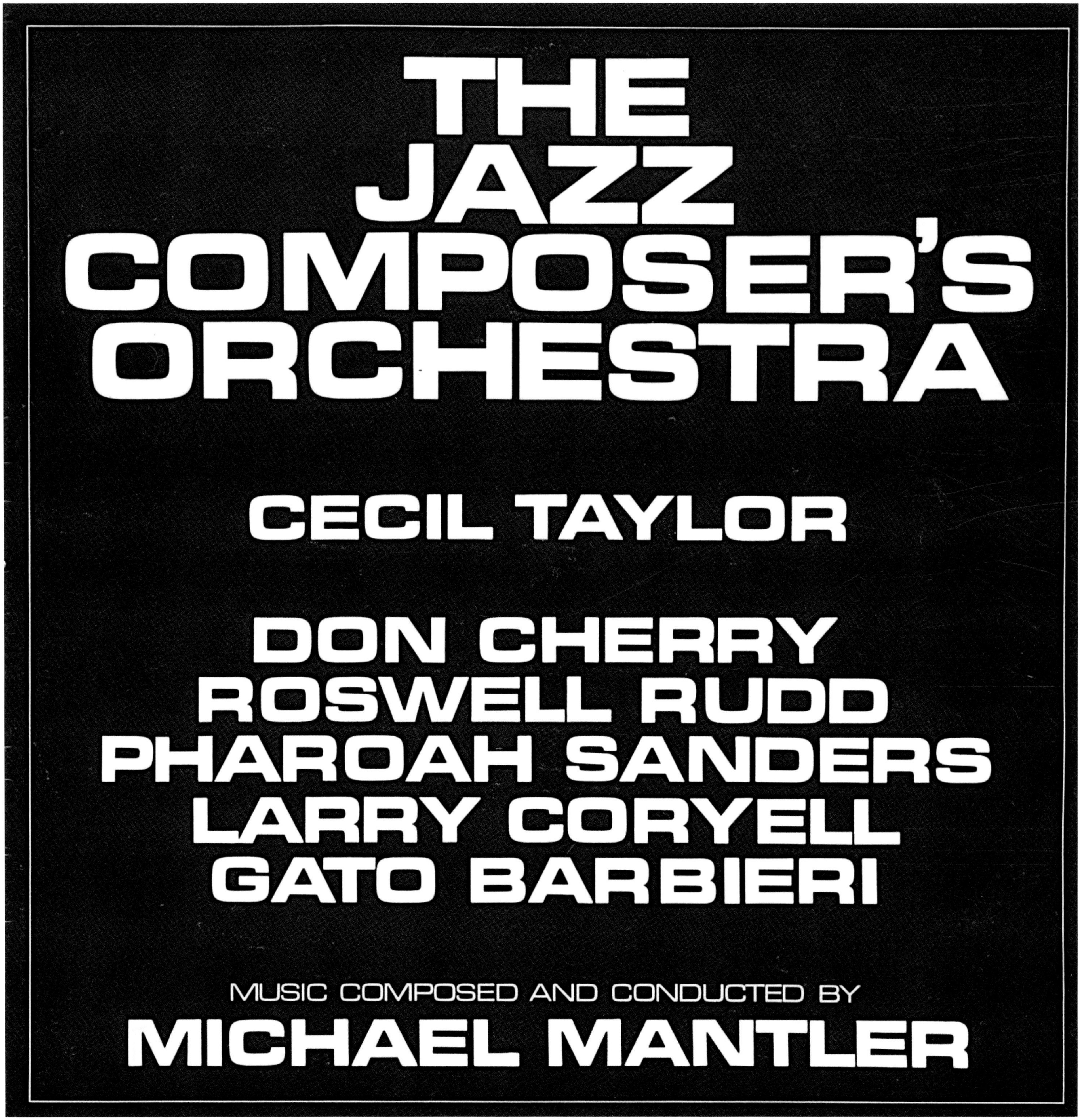

THE JAZZ COMPOSER'S ORCHESTRA

CECIL TAYLOR

DON CHERRY
ROSWELL RUDD
PHAROAH SANDERS
LARRY CORYELL
GATO BARBIERI

MUSIC COMPOSED AND CONDUCTED BY
MICHAEL MANTLER

THE JAZZ COMPOSER'S ORCHESTRA The Jazz Composer's Orchestra **JCOA Records** 1968
Cover, Design & Layout Paul McDonough

OFAMFA Children Of The Sun **Universal Justice Records** 1972

SUN RA AND THE ARKESTRA Cosmo Sun Connection **El Saturn Records** 1985

THE BRASS COMPANY Colors **Strata-East Records** 1975
Cover Artwork by Sandra Williams

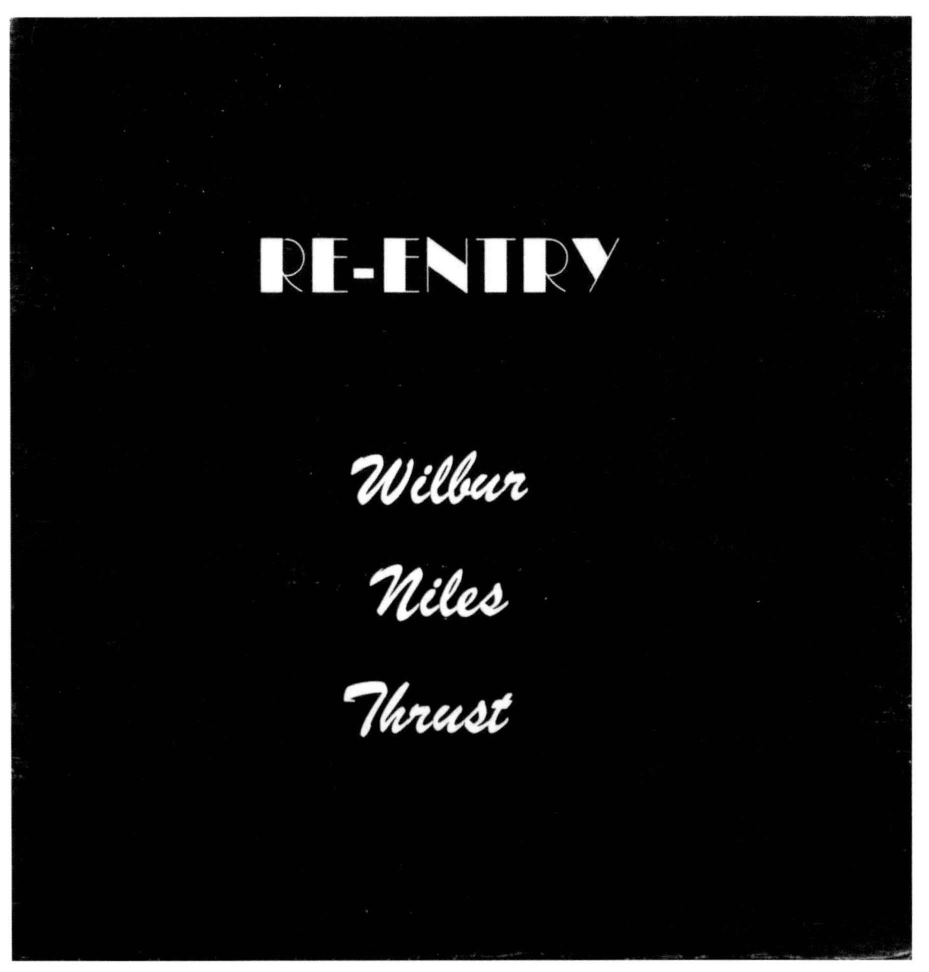

WILBUR NILES THRUST Re-Entry **Plum Place Records** 1987

CLEVE POZAR Solo Percussion **CSP** 1974

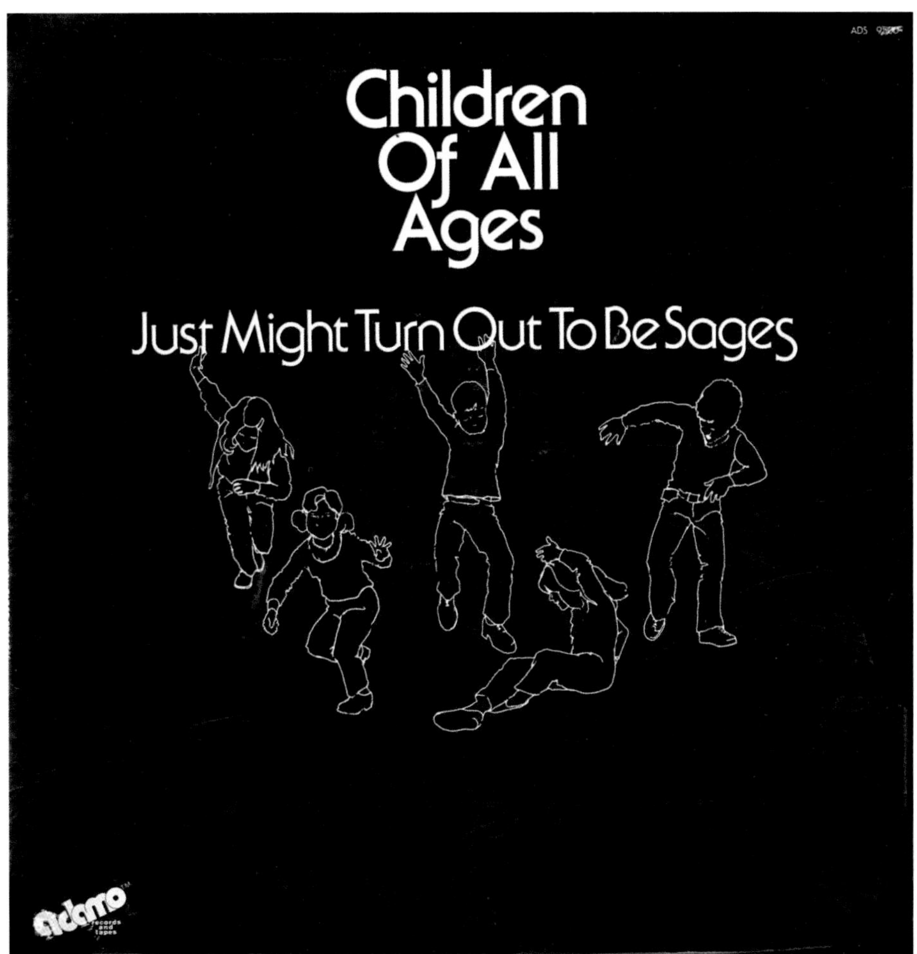

CHILDREN OF ALL AGES JUST MIGHT TURN OUT TO BE SAGES
Adamo Records and Tapes 1976

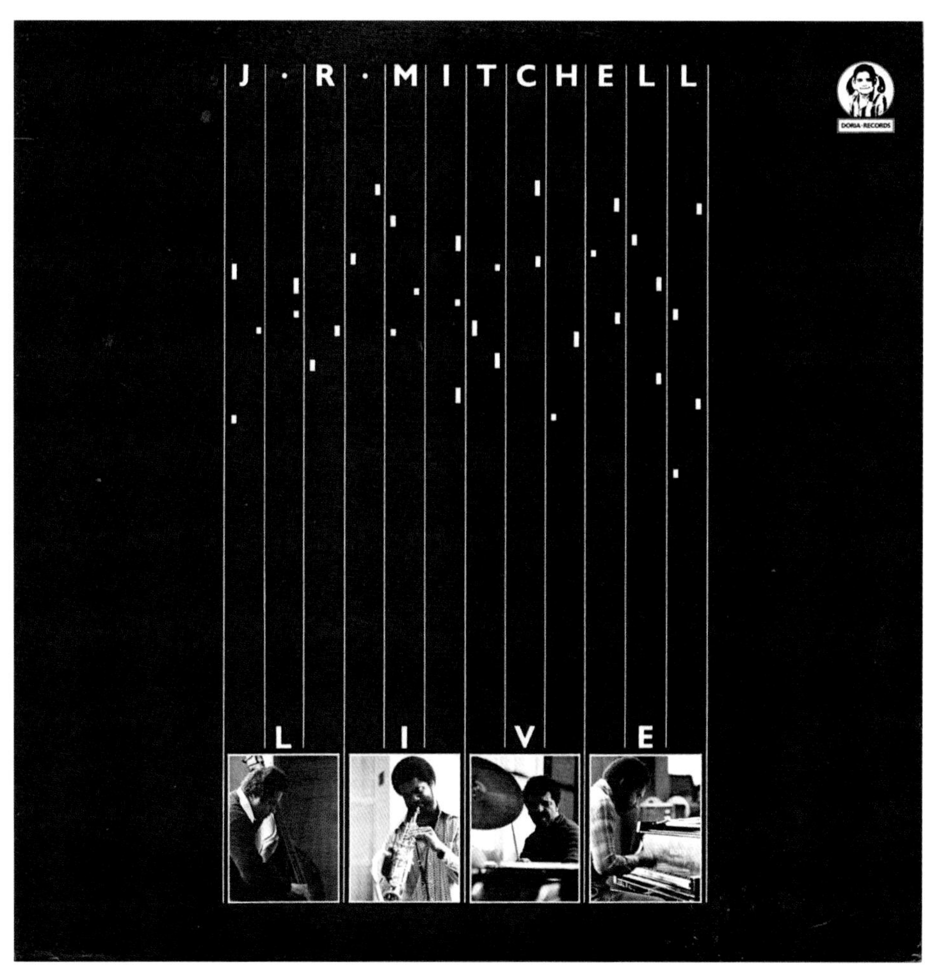

J R MITCHELL Live **Dorla Records** 1980

DERWN HOLDER'S ASTRAL VISIONS Time Open **Neen Records** 1977

NDIKHO KABA AND THE NATIVES s/t **Trilyte** 1971
Design by Eddie Horan **Art Conception by** Nomusa Xaba

PAUL NASH A Jazz Composer's Ensemble **Revelation Records** 1979
Cover Drawing by Ruth Tannenbaum

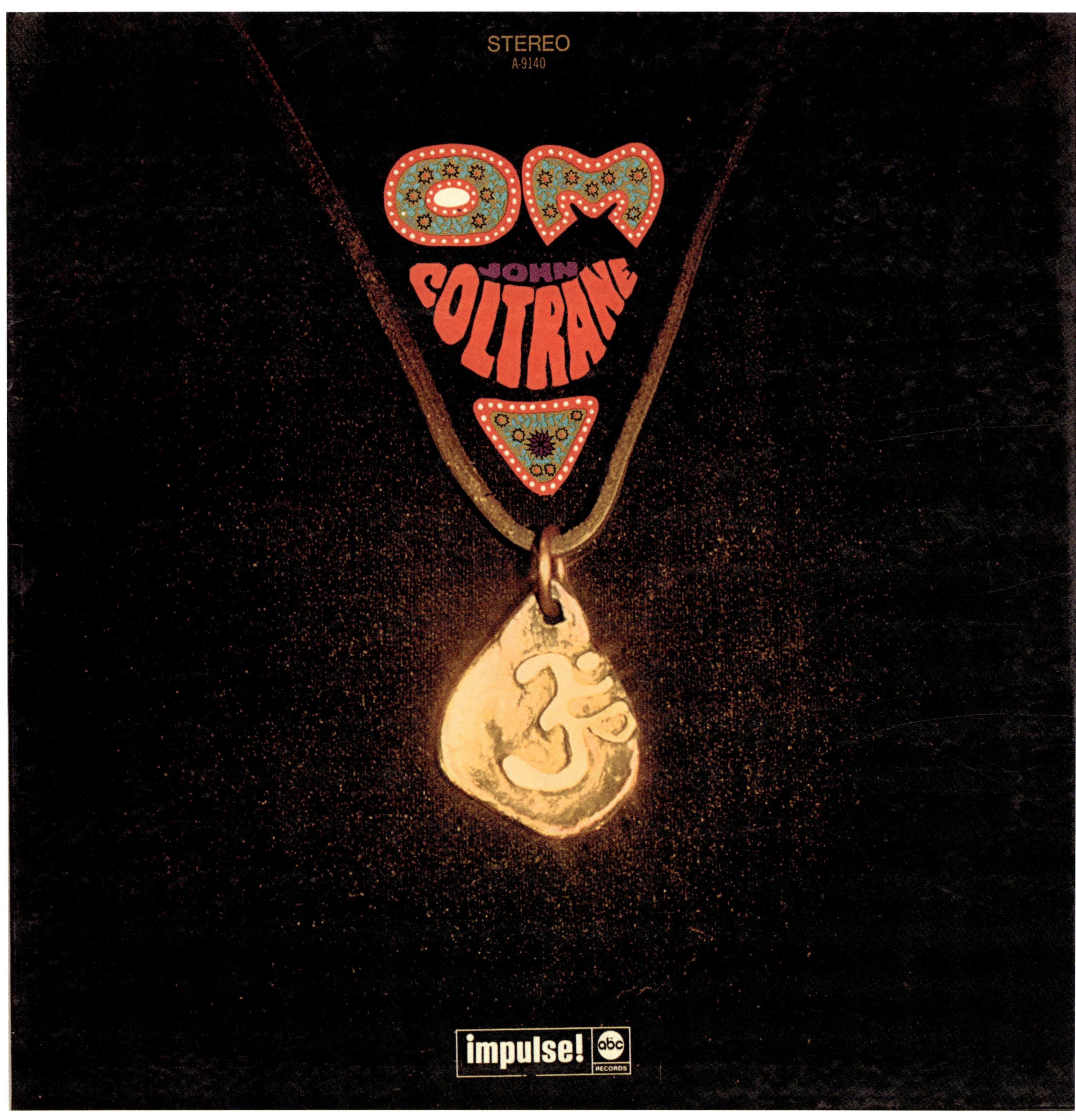

JOHN COLTRANE Om **Impulse! Records** 1967
Cover Artwork by Robert & Barbara Flynn

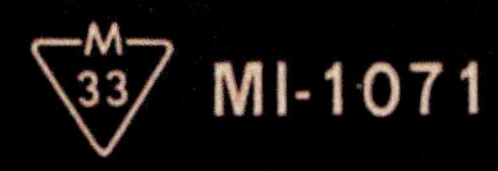

CECIL TAYLOR QUARTET & THE GIGI GRYCE - DONALD BYRD JAZZ LABORATORY At Newport '57 **Verve** (Originally issued on American Recording Society, 1957)

MARION BROWN Solo Saxophone **Sweet Earth Records** 1977
Painting by Nelson Stevens

THE AWAKENING Brand New Feeling **Ovation Records** 1976
Design by Herb Bruce **Graphics by** Bob Dorobiala

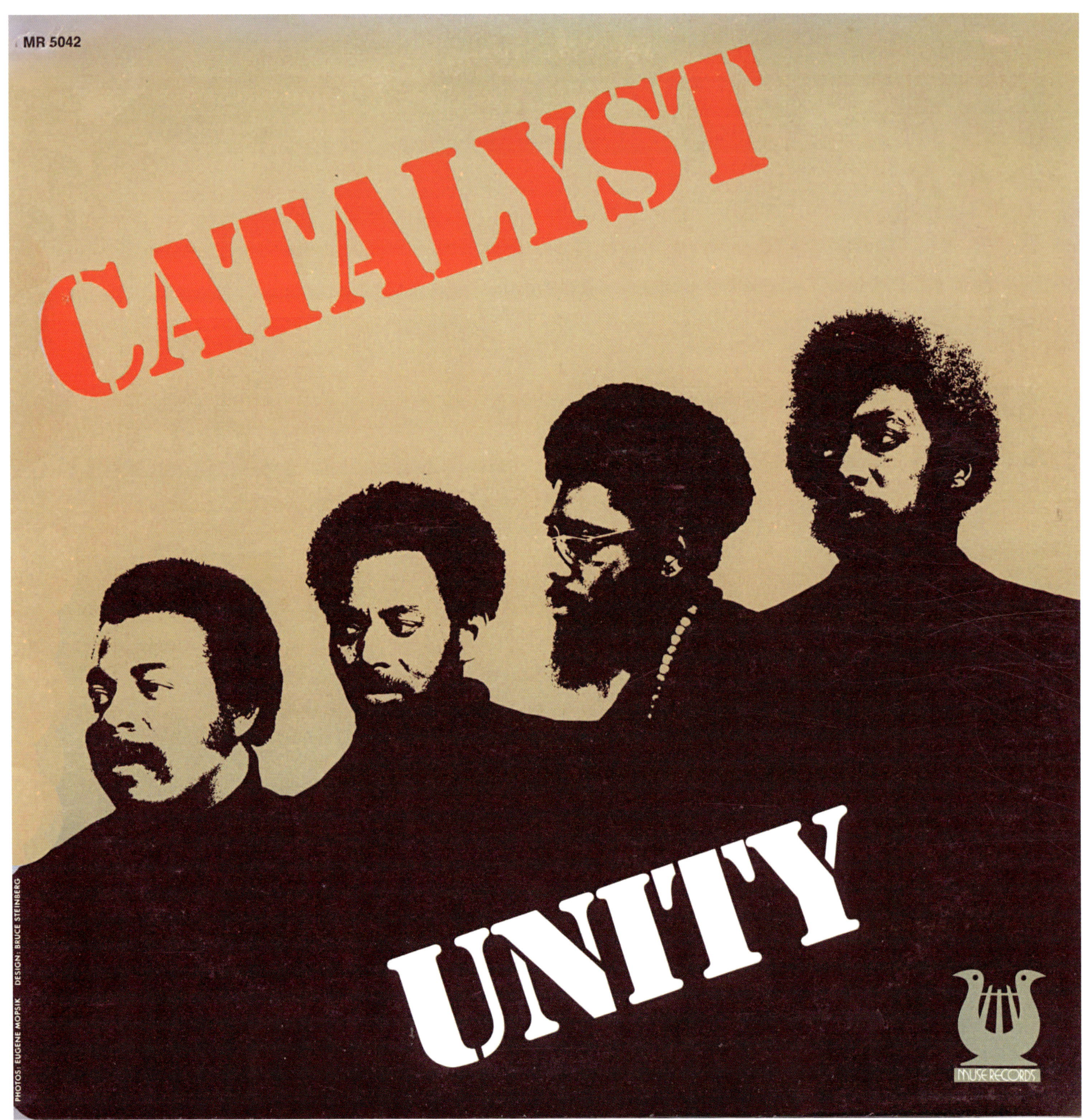

CATALYST Unity **Muse Records** 1974
Design by Bruce Steinberg **Photography by** Eugene Mopsik

CLEVELAND EATON Plenty Good Eaton **Black Jazz Records** 1975
Photography by Howard D. Simmons

In 1967, Fernand Boruso, Jean-Luc Young and Jean Georgakarakos founded BYG (an acronym of their names). Boruso had previously worked for Pierre Barouh's 'Saravah' label and Young for Barclay. Boruso left the following year.

In the summer of 1969, BYG invited some musicians to Paris for recording sessions. These included Don Cherry, Archie Shepp, The Art Ensemble of Chicago and Anthony Braxton among others. In July of that year, the Pan-African music festival took place in Algiers. Archie Shepp and a number of the American avant-garde flew over from the USA to perform there.

Claude Decloo was editor of Actuel a French avant-garde and cultural magazine, and also a drummer in The Full Moon Ensemble. The Algiers Festival was captured by Actuel photographer Jacques Bisceglia. After the festival, with Claude Decloo as A&R, a number of these musicians were invited to Paris.

Clifford Thornton, Grachan Moncur III, Sunny Murray, Dave Burrell, Alan Silva and others came and recorded in Paris. A month later, Jimmy Lyons and Andrew Cyrille also arrived from touring with Cecil Taylor. This resulted in a marathon set of recording sessions taking place which created the catalogue of BYG/Actuel. All the albums featured striking graphic cover designs by Claude Caudron.

A planned five-day, 24-hour BYG/Actuel concert was planned for the fall of 1969 in Paris featuring many of these artists alongside underground rock and psychedelia groups, however the event was moved to Amougies on the Belgian border at the last minute. Nevertheless 20,000 French, Belgian and German fans came. Frank Zappa introduced performances by Art Ensemble, Grachan Moncur III, Don Cherry, Sunny Murray, Archie Shepp, Pharoah Sanders playing alongside Pink Floyd, Captain Beefheart, The Nice, Yes and The Pretty Things.

BYG released 52LPs between 1969 and 1972 before the label closed the following year. Jean-Luc Young set up Charly Records (who have recently reissued the catalogue on vinyl once more) and Jean Georgakarakos launched Celluloid. The creation of the BYG/Actuel catalogue was a defining move in establishing the American avant-garde in Europe and resulted in the opportunity for these artists to work with a number of European producers, in Paris, France and across Europe over the ensuing years.

ART ENSEMBLE OF CHICAGO Message to Our Folks **BYG Records** 1969 **Photography by** Horace

ARCHIE SHEPP Blasé **BYG Records** 1969 **Photography by** Jacques Bisceglia

GRACAN MONCUR III New Africa **BYG Records** 1969 **Photography by** Jacques Bisceglia

sonny sharrock
monkey - pockie - boo

SONNY SHARROCK Monkey-Pockie-Boo **BYG Records** 1970
Photography by Jacques Bisceglia

MARION BROWN Soul Eyes **Baystate** 1979
Photography by Shingo Satoh

HANNIBAL AND THE SUNRISE ORCHESTRA Live In Lausanne **Baystate Records** 1978
Photography by Matsuhiro Sugawara **Design by** Tadao Aoyagi

DAVID WERTMAN SUN ENSEMBLE Earthly Delights **Sweet Earth Records** 1978
Artwork by David Wertman

Spontaneous Combustion

SPONTANEOUS COMBUSTION All The Time **Spontaneous Combustion Inc.** c.1980

5 7 6 1 7 1 1 5 5 5
(28) 1 + (15) 6 = 43 – 7

REVOLUTIONARY ENSEMBLE

164 = 11 tc

2 6 3 4 5 2 5 3 4 2 3
(22) 4 + (17) 8 = 39 – 3
2 5 6 7 3 6 4 1 7 5 1 2 1 5 5 3 5 4 2 3 5
(50) 5 + (32) 5 = 82 – 1

SIRONE LEROY JENKINS JEROME COOPER

enja 3003

REVOLUTIONARY ENSEMBLE s/t **Enja** 1977
Photography by A. Haase **Design by** Weber / Winckelmann **Artwork by** Jerome Cooper

THE GIFT OF LOVE

SAM SANDERS & VISIONS

SAM SANDERS & VISIONS The Gift of Love **That African Lady** 1983
Art Direction by Allan Colding **Photography by** Leni Sinclair

BLACK ARTHUR BLYTHE
BUSH BABY
THE ADELPHI JAZZ LINE

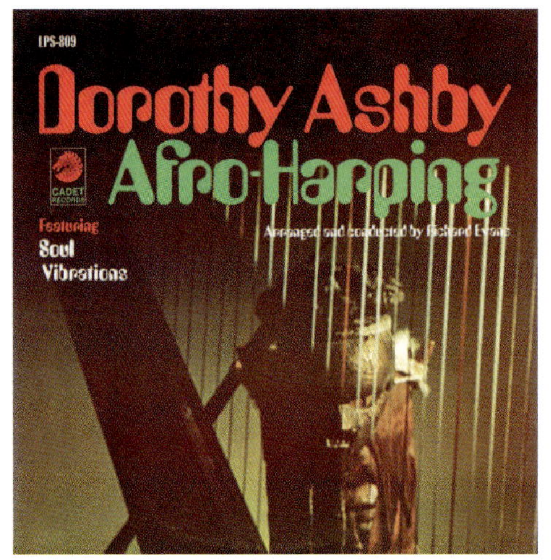
LPS-809
Dorothy Ashby
Afro-Harping
CADET RECORDS
Featuring
Soul Vibrations

CARTER JEFFERSON THE RISE OF ATLANTIS
TERUMASA HINO / HARRY WHITAKER / CLINT HOUSTON / VICTOR LEWIS / SHUNZO ONO / JOHN HICKS

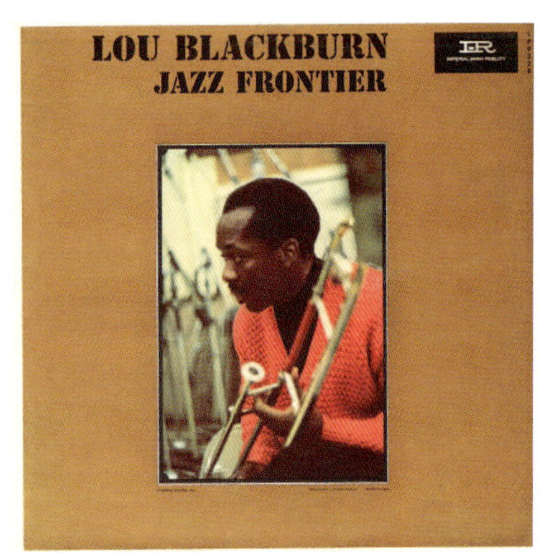
LOU BLACKBURN
JAZZ FRONTIER

MUHAL RICHARD ABRAMS
THINGS TO COME FROM THOSE NOW GONE

ORNETTE COLEMAN
TWINS
SD 1588

Fred Anderson Quintet
MOERS MUSIC
ANOTHER PLACE
Featuring Billy Brimfield, George Lewis, Brian Smith, Hank Drake

CARLOS FRANZETTI
New York Toccata

INTRODUCING: DUKE EDWARDS and
the young ones
IS IT TOO LATE?

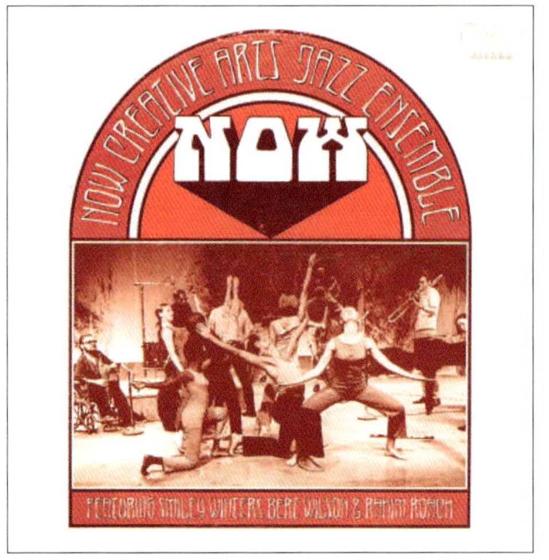
NOW CREATIVE ARTS JAZZ ENSEMBLE
NOW

contours
sam rivers
BLUE NOTE
FREDDIE HUBBARD HERBIE HANCOCK RON CARTER JOE CHAMBERS

SONNY SIMMONS
MANHATTAN EGOS
STEREO

THE SEVENTH SON
MALACHI THOMPSON

DON CHERRY
HEAR & NOW

DEWEY REDMAN
COINCIDE
impulse!

THE LEON THOMAS ALBUM

RAHSAAN ROLAND KIRK
RAHSAAN RAHSAAN

Cornelius Bumpus
A Clear View

FUCHSIA SWING SONG SAM RIVERS

TWO IS ONE
CHARLES ROUSE

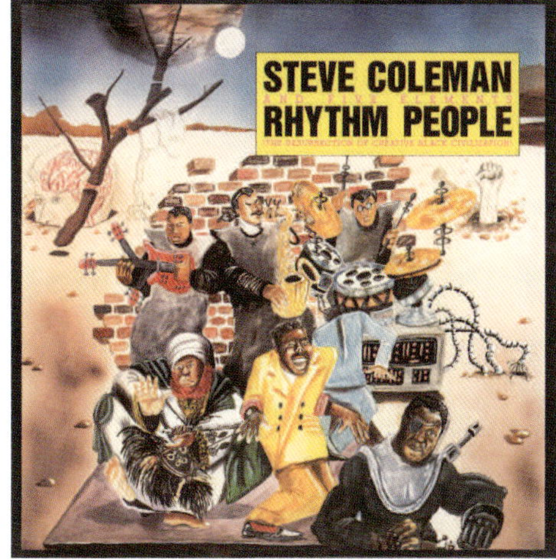
STEVE COLEMAN
RHYTHM PEOPLE

STEREO
TEXTURES
THE BILL DOBBINS JAZZ ORCHESTRA

JAZZ from SAN FRANCISCO
THE PAT BRITT QUINTET

STATLER RECORDS
presents
AFRO-CUBAN JAZZ
ETHNIC-
FEVER
by
FRANK HATCHET
L.P. No. 1199

Billy Bang and Charles Tyler
LIVE
Green Space

L.P. 9040
ETHNIC DANCES
OF BLACK PEOPLE
AROUND THE WORLD
CREATED BY
MARIE BROOKS

Just a Little Boy
The Dave Henrie
Quartet + Charlotte

Raphael
Roberto Miguel Miranda
Virallio Figueroa

DIVINE HORSEMEN
THE VOODOO GODS OF HAITI

ALBERT DAILEY THE DAY AFTER THE DAWN

shades of joy

ROSCOE
MITCHELL
DUETS WITH
ANTHONY BRAXTON
SACKVILLE STEREO 3016

ROSCOE MITCHELL Duets With Anthony Braxton **Sackville Recordings** 1978
Design and Photography by Bill Smith

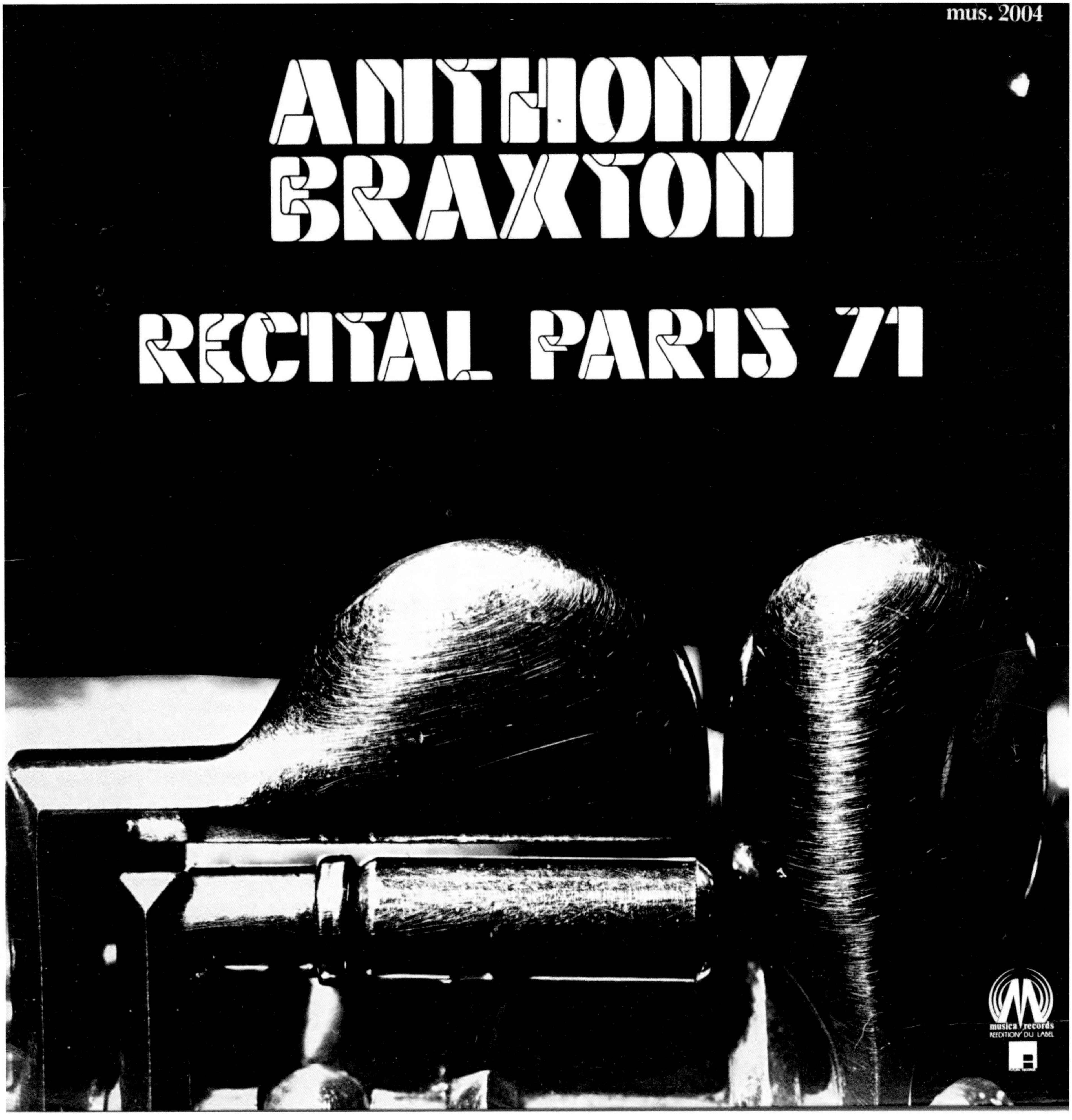

ANTHONY BRAXTON

RECITAL PARIS 71

musica records
REEDITION DU LABEL

ANTHONY BRAXTON Recital Paris 71 **Futura Records** 1971
Design and Photography by Jean-Marc Decker

STEREO 2003

BYARD LANCASTER

IT'S NOT UP TO US

BYARD LANCASTER It's Not Up To Us **Vortex Records** 1968
Cover Artwork by Marvin Israel **Photography by** Lee Friedlander and Michael Wilderman

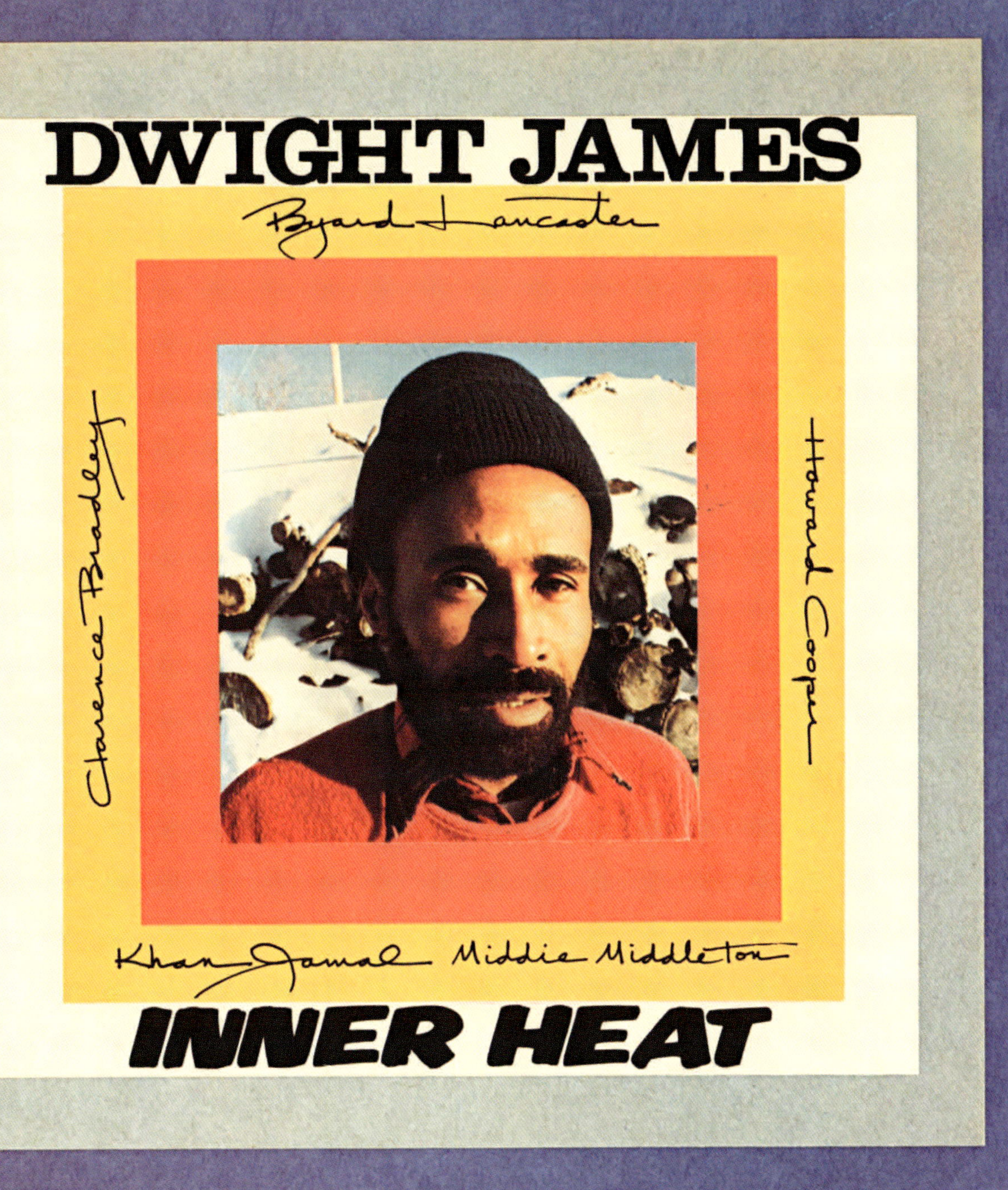

DWIGHT JAMES Inner Heat **Cadence Jazz Records** 1983
Artwork and Photography by Bob Rusch **Layout by** Susan Rusch **Lithography by** Kathy Joyce and Rusch

ANDREW McPHERSON At Smedley's Squalor **Records** 1965

ROBERT ROCKWELL III Androids **Celebration Records** 1974
Cover Artwork by Bill Berg

WALT DICKERSON & SUN RA Visions **SteepleChase** 1979
Design by Per Grunnet

LUTHER THOMAS CREATIVE ENSEMBLE Funky Donkey
Circle Records 1977 **Photography by** Rudolf Kreis

HENRY THREADGILL X-75 Volume 1 **Arista Novus** 1979
Art Direction by Donn Davenport **Photography by** Mel Dixon

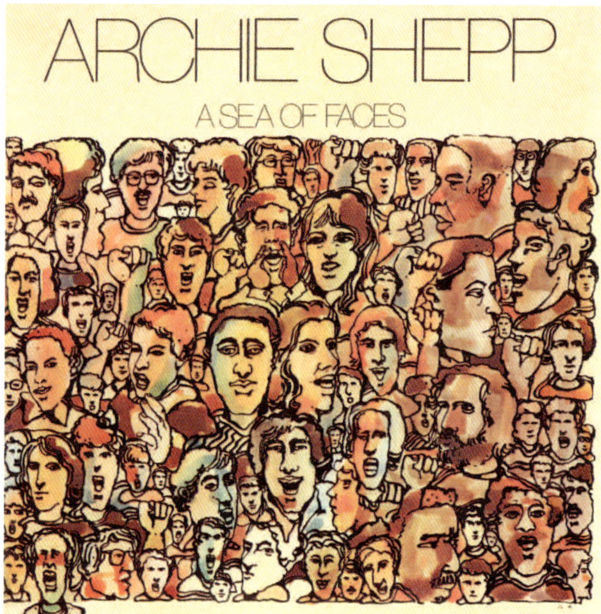

ARCHIE SHEPP A Sea Of Faces **Black Saint** 1975
Design by Ariel Soule

ROY BROOKS Beat **Workshop Jazz** 1964
Cover Artwork by Wallace Mead & Bernard Yeszin

LEROY VINNEGAR The Kid **PBR International** 1974
Cover Artwork by Nancy Buchanan

THE ERNIE SCOTT TRIO In Concert **Media IV Records** 1970

BOBBY RODRIGUEZ Simply Macrame **Jazz Men Records** 1973 **Design by** Armondo Romo and Chico Smith

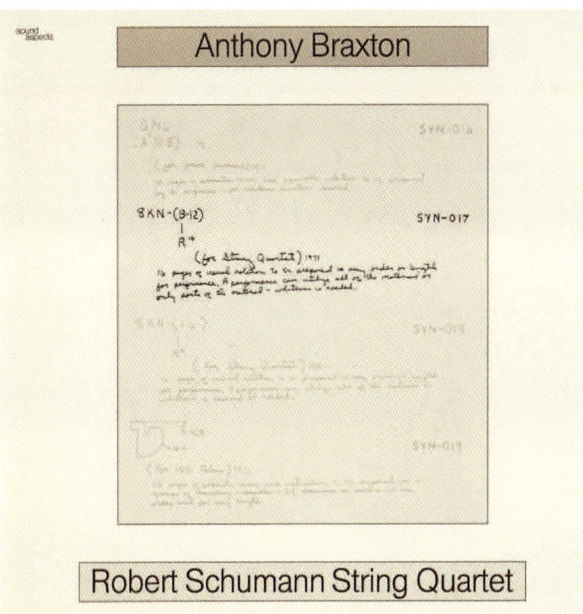

ANTHONY BRAXTON/ROBERT SCHUMANN STRING QUARTET String Quartet Sound **Aspects Records** 1986 **Design by** Margit-Lämmle

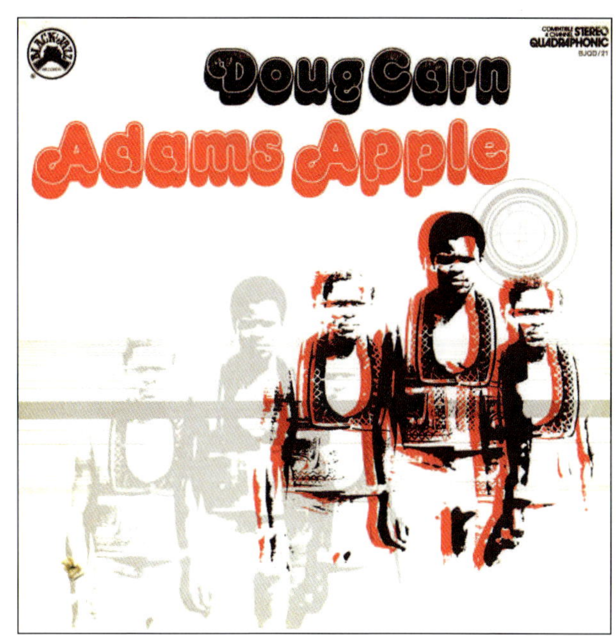

DOUG CARN Adams Apple **Black Jazz Records** 1974 **Cover Artwork by** Jerry Napier **Graphics by** Grafica Studio, Inc.

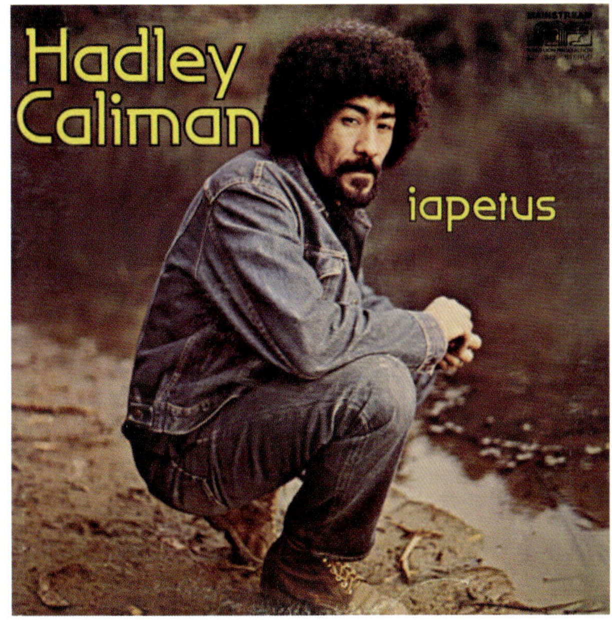

HADLEY CALIMAN Iapetus **Mainstream Records** 1974 **Design by** Ruby Mazur's Art Department

ELVIN JONES & McCOY TYNER QUINTET Love & Peace **Trio Records** 1982 **Design by** Watanabe Jr. **Photography by** Stephen A. Weiss

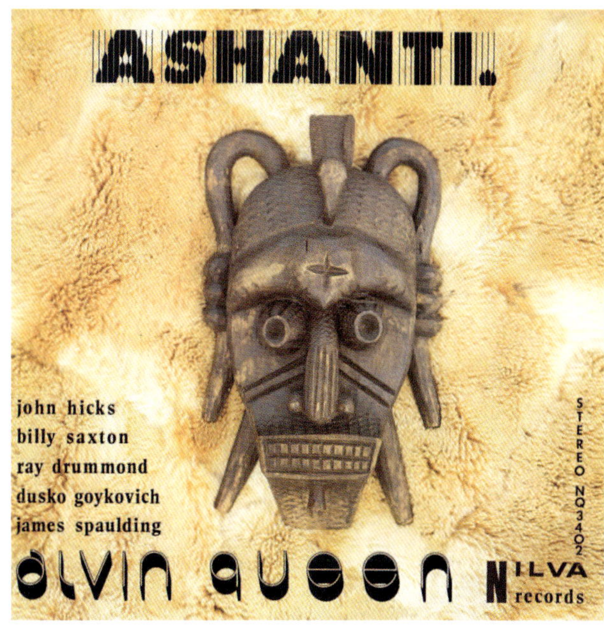

ALVIN QUEEN Ashanti **Nilva Records** 1981 **Design by** Julius Kubik

WOODY SHAW Little Red's Fantasy **Muse Records** 1978 **Photography by** Yasuhisa Yoneda

GHALIB GHALLAB Let Me Love You **Shabazz Records & Tapes** 1987 **Photography by** Jerome Simmons **Graphics by** MakeReady Inc.

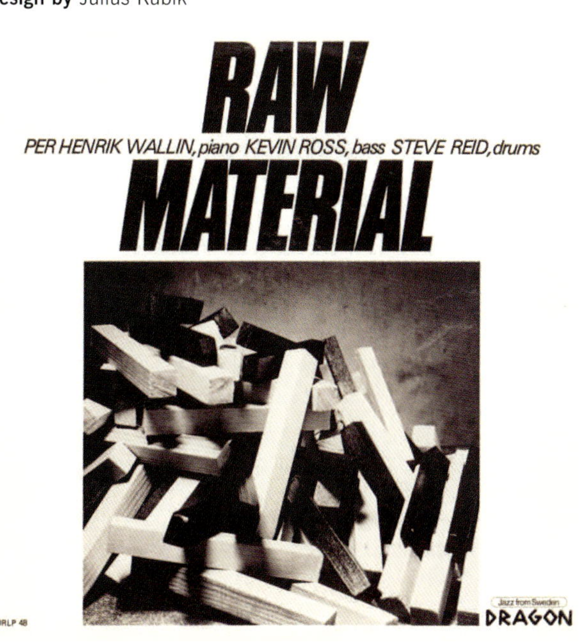

PER HENRIK WALLIN / KEVIN ROSS / STEVE REID Raw Material **Dragon** 1983 **Design by** Tandemkreatörerna **Photography by** Pawel Lucki

SUN RA AND HIS ARKESTRA Super Sonic Jazz **El Saturn Records** 1957

WILLIAM PARKER Through Acceptance Of The Mystery Peace **Centering Records** 1980
Artwork by Ana F. Esquivel **Photography by** Pamela Read

MUSE RECORDS

Muse Records was set up by Joe Fields in New York in 1972. Fields was a record man and had previously worked at Prestige (with Bob Weinstock), Colombia, Sue Records (owned by Juggy Murray), Buddah (with Neil Bogart, who would later start the disco label Casablanca) and Verve (with Creed Taylor). Fields also ran two other labels – Cobblestone, which was initially a division of Buddah Records, and Onyx, which reissued older material. Without the fanfare of larger labels such as Blue Note, CTI etc, Muse quietly released over 200 high quality jazz albums through the 1970s. The catalogue includes powerful deep, spiritual jazz, Brazilian and heavyweight fusion from known and unknown artists alike - Carlos Garnett, Catalyst, Neal Creque, Hermeto Pascoal, Norman Connors, Roy Brooks, Dom un Romao, Mark Murphy, Chick Corea and more.

Many of the sleeves were designed by graphic designer, painter, and photographer Ron Warwell. The artwork managed to give the label a satisfyingly 'diverse yet cohesive' look, perfectly in keeping with the music on the label. Warwell was also a painter and created the afro-centric paintings which adorn Carlos Garnett's albums 'Journey to Enlightenment' and 'Cosmos Nucleus' and the Visitors' 'Motherland' cover as well as others featured throughout this book. Another regular designer was Hal Wilson.

At the end of the 1980s the label stopped pressing vinyl and moved over to compact disc. In 1993, Fields sold the label to 32 Records, owned by record producer Joel Dorn and Robert Miller.

RICHARD DAVIS Dealin' **Muse Records** 1974

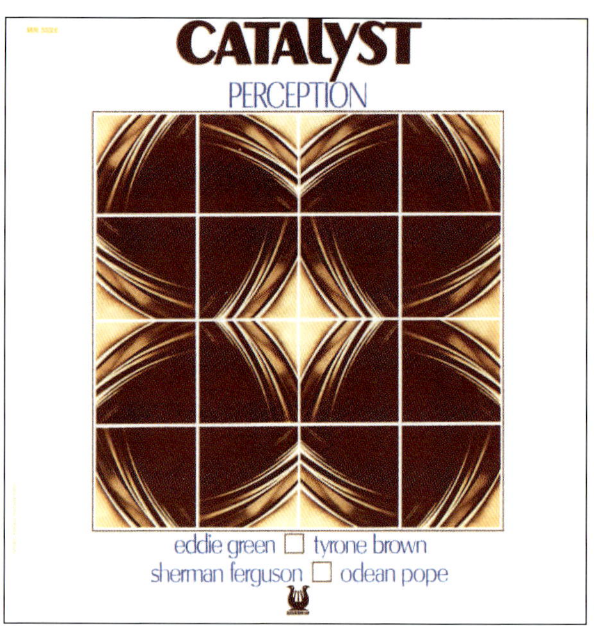

CATALYST Perception **Muse Records** 1973
Design and Photography by Spencer Zahn

ROBIN KENYATTA Beggars and Stealers **Muse Records** 1977
Cover Design and Photography by Price Givens

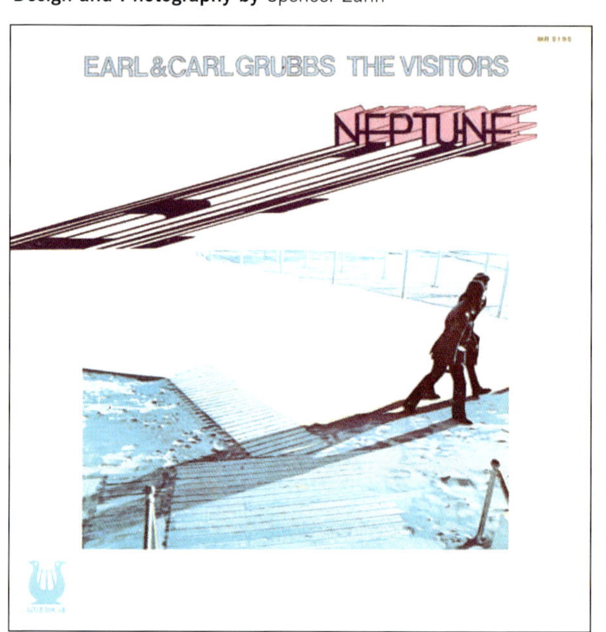

THE VISITORS EARL & CARL GRUBBS Neptune **Muse Records** 1980
Design by Ron Warwell

CECIL BROOKS III The Collective **Muse Records** 1989

WALTER BISHOP JR Vally Land **Muse Records** 1976
Art Direction, Design and Photography by Hal Wilson

CARLOS GARNETT Let This Melody Ring On **Muse Records** 1975

JAMES MOODY Never Again! **Muse Records** 1972

THE VISITORS EARL & CARL GRUBBS Motherland **Muse Records** 1976 **Cover Artwork by** Ron Warwell

RICHARD DAVIS Epistrophy & Now's The Time **Muse Records** 1973 **Design and Photography by** Don Schlitten

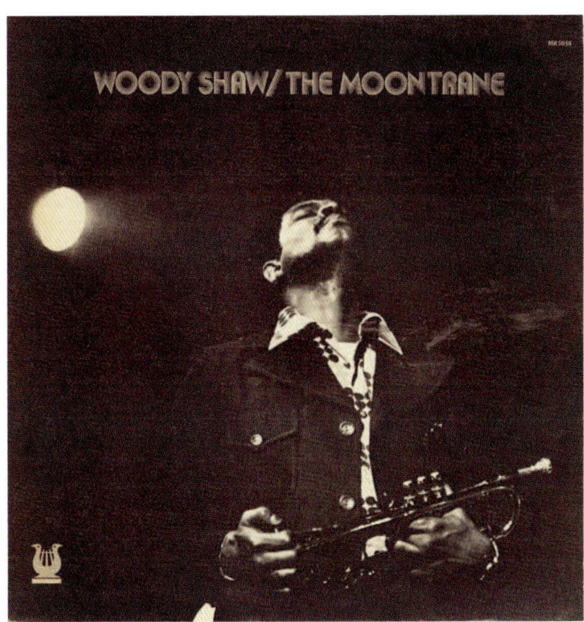

WOODY SHAW The Moontrane **Muse Records** 1975 **Design and Photography by** Ron Warwell

CARLOS GARNETT Black Love **Muse Records** 1974 **Photography by** Clarence Eastmond

CARLOS GARNETT The New Love **Muse Records** 1978 **Design and Photography by** Ron Warwell

WOODY SHAW WITH ANTHONY BRAXTON The Iron Men **Muse Records** 1981 **Cover Artwork by** Stephanie Blumenthal

JOE CHAMBERS The Almoravid **Muse Records** 1974

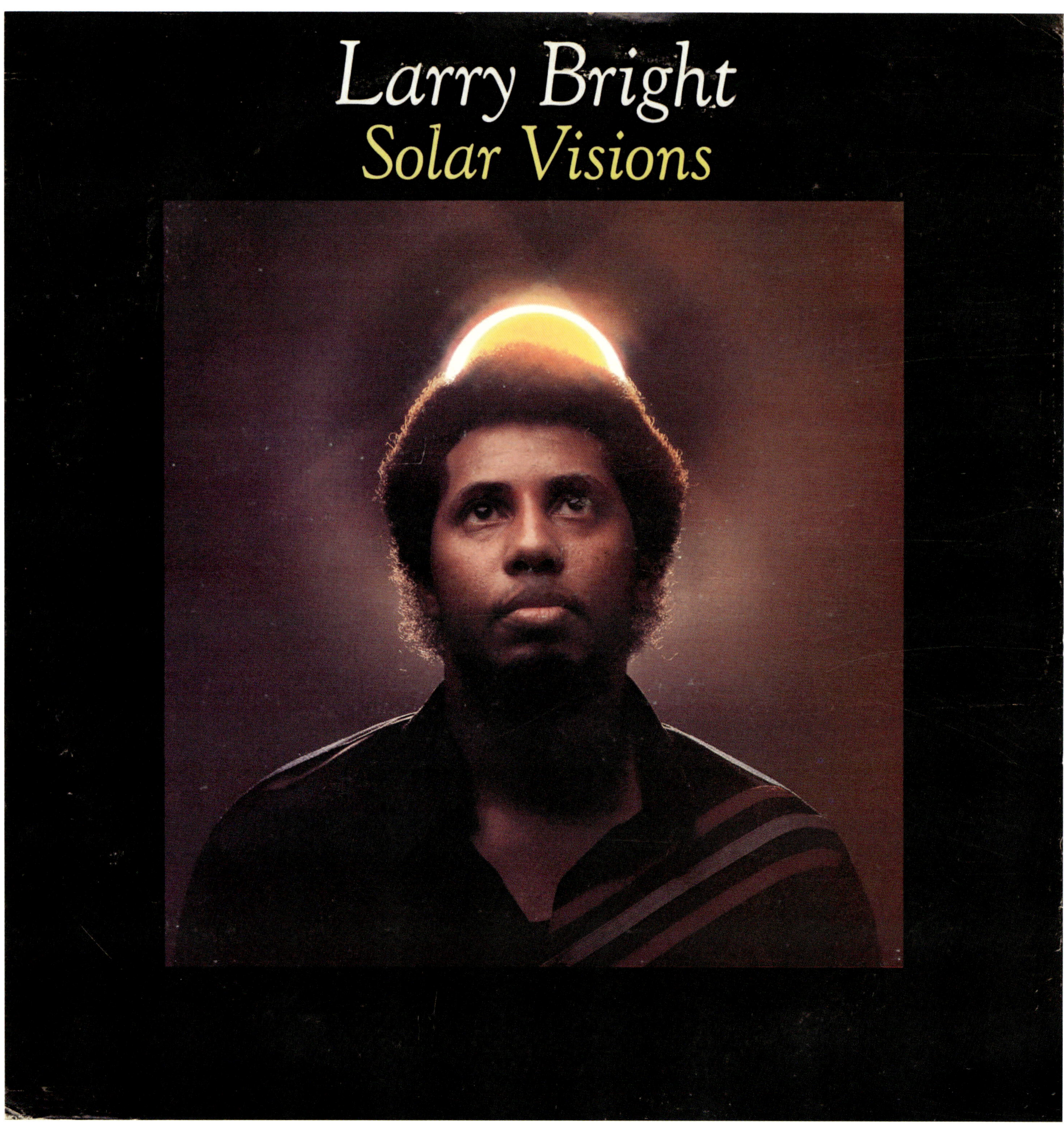

LARRY BRIGHT Solar Visions **Crosswind Records** 1978
Photography by Allen Polansky

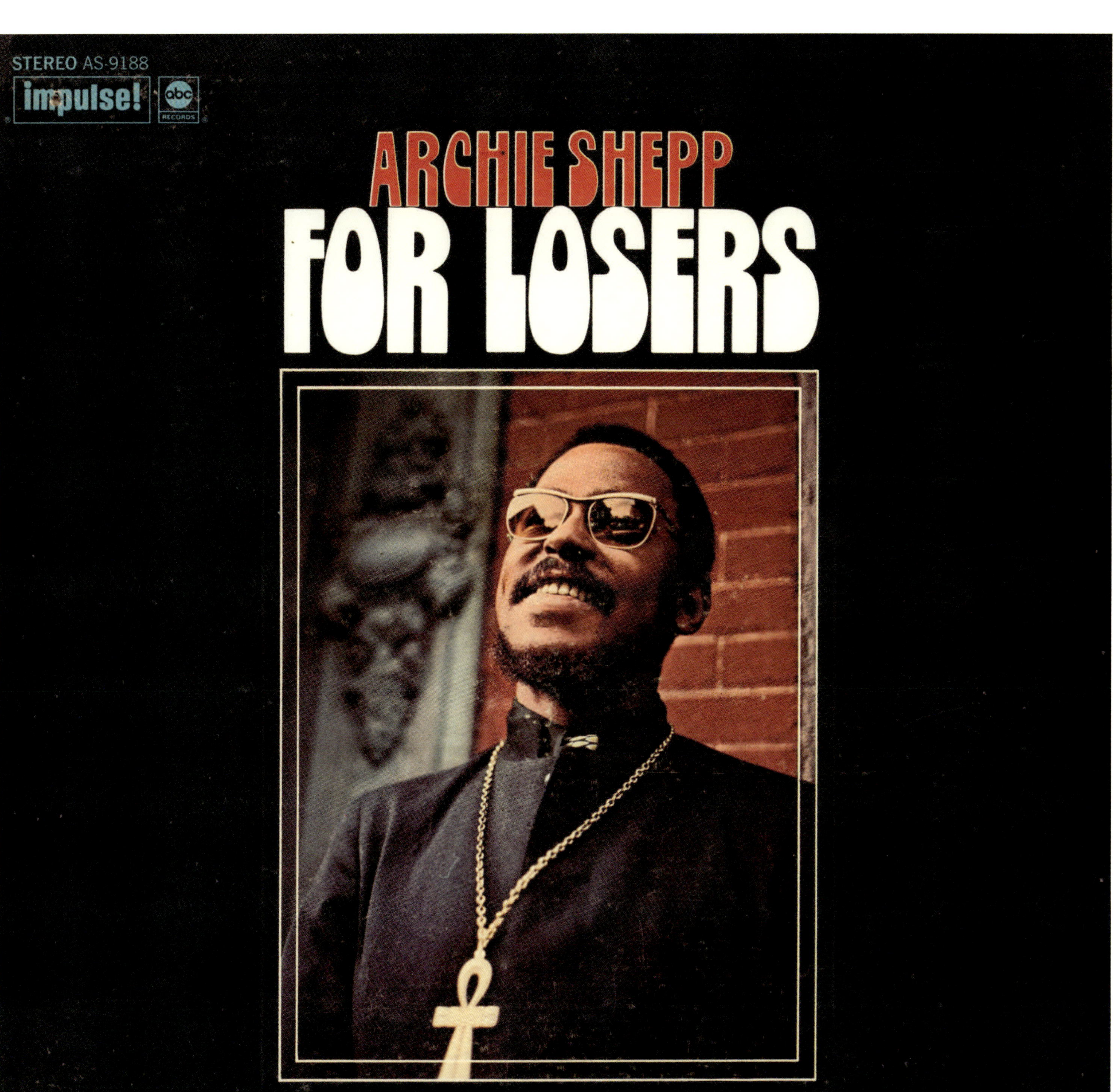

ARCHIE SHEPP For Losers **Impulse**! 1970
Photography by Chuck Stewart **Design by** George Whiteman

CECIL TAYLOR Great Paris Concert 2 **Freedom** 1980 (Originally issued on BYG, 1973)
Photography and Design by K. Abe

BILLY BANG'S SURVIVAL ENSEMBLE New York Collage **Anima Records** 1978
Design by B & J Designs **Photography by** John Dent

KENNY GILL What Was What Is What Will Be **Racoon / Warner Bros.** 1971

WILL CRITTENDON AND AFRO-JAZZ ENSEMBLE Message From The Third **World Raynard** 1968
Photography by Tom Harris

ENJA RECORDS

Matthias Winckelmann and Horst Weber founded Enja Records in Munich in 1971. The intention behind the label was to focus on modern European jazz music (ENJA was meant to stand for European New Jazz) but in fact they immediately began working with a set of international artists working in Germany. The label launched with releases by Mal Waldron, Music Inc (Charles Tolliver and Stanley Cowell, co-founders of Strata-East), South African pianist Dollar brand, German trombonist Albert Mangelsdorff and Japanese trumpeter Teremasa Hino.

Many more releases followed from cutting-edge American jazz artists Elvin Jones, Randy Weston, Bobby Hutcherson, Archie Shepp, Leroy Jenkins and Cecil Taylor. In 1986, the owners split their partnership and went on to create two separate labels: ENJA Records Matthias Winckelmann and ENJA Records Horst Weber. Today, the ENJA catalogues are reunited, with the label now in business for over 50 years.

MAL WALDRON JIMMY WOODE PIERRE FAVRE Black Glory **Enja Records** 1971 **Design by** Weber and Winckelmann **Photography by** Josef Werkmeister

MAL WALDRON REGGIE WORKMAN BILLY HIGGINS Up Popped The Devil **Enja Records** 1974 **Design by** Weber and Winckelmann **Photography by** Cairati

DOLLAR BRAND XAHURI African Sketchbook **Enja Records** 1973 **Design by** Weber and Winckelmann **Photography by** Josef Werkmeister

enja SFX-10709

IMPACT

MUSIC INC /

CHARLES TOLLIVER

STANLEY COWELL

RON MATHEWSON

ALVIN QUEEN

RECORDED LIVE

AT THE DOMICILE

MUSIC INC / CHARLES TOLLIVER STANLEY COWELL RON MATHEWSON ALVIN QUEEN Impact **Enja Records** 1972
Design by Weber and Winckelmann **Photography by** Josef Werkmeister

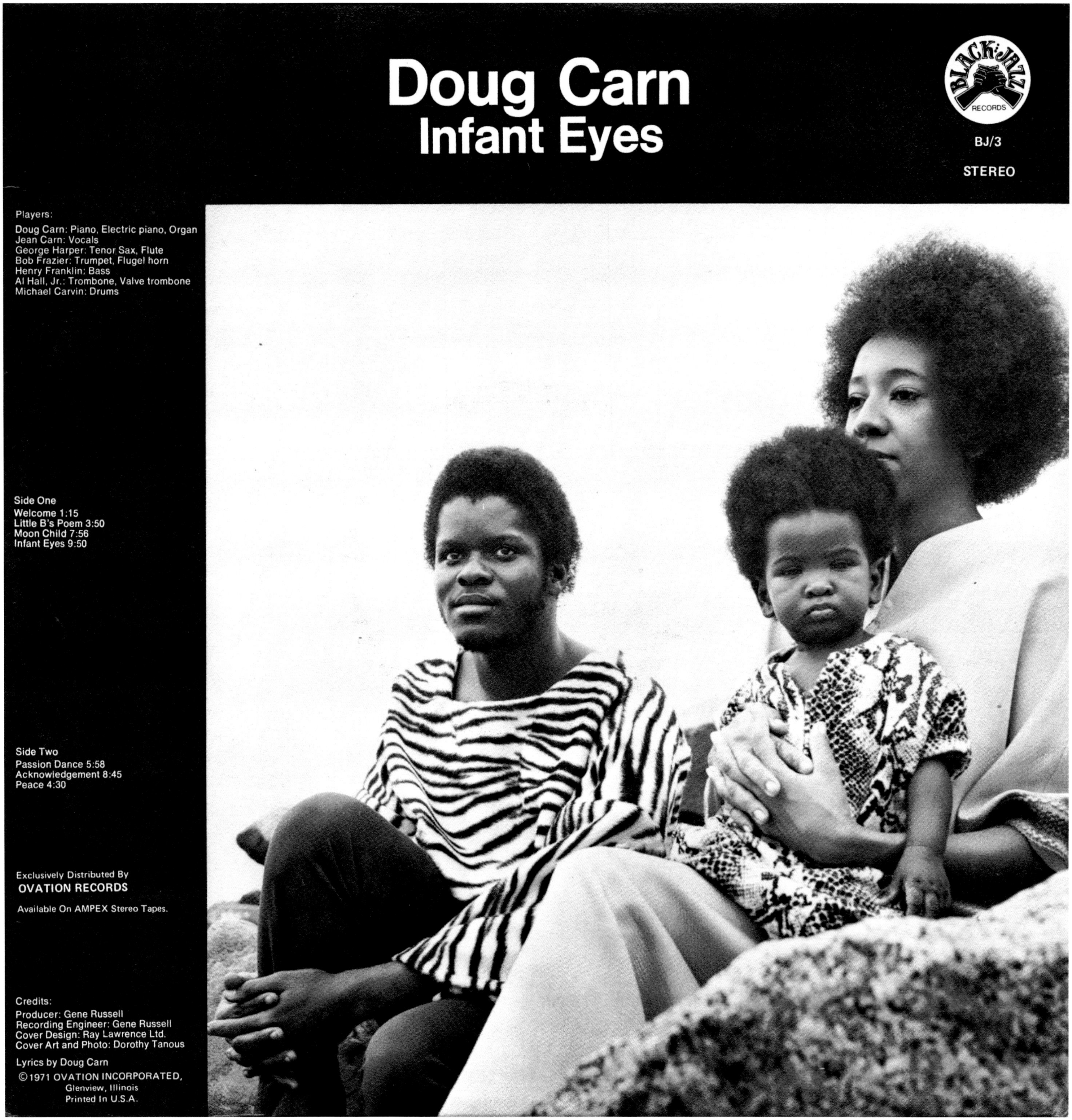

Doug Carn
Infant Eyes

BJ/3

STEREO

Players:

Doug Carn: Piano, Electric piano, Organ
Jean Carn: Vocals
George Harper: Tenor Sax, Flute
Bob Frazier: Trumpet, Flugel horn
Henry Franklin: Bass
Al Hall, Jr.: Trombone, Valve trombone
Michael Carvin: Drums

Side One

Welcome 1:15
Little B's Poem 3:50
Moon Child 7:56
Infant Eyes 9:50

Side Two

Passion Dance 5:58
Acknowledgement 8:45
Peace 4:30

Exclusively Distributed By
OVATION RECORDS

Available On AMPEX Stereo Tapes.

Credits:

Producer: Gene Russell
Recording Engineer: Gene Russell
Cover Design: Ray Lawrence Ltd.
Cover Art and Photo: Dorothy Tanous

Lyrics by Doug Carn

©1971 OVATION INCORPORATED,
Glenview, Illinois
Printed In U.S.A.

DOUG CARN Infant Eyes **Black Jazz Records** 1971
Photography by Dorothy Tanous **Design by** Ray Lawrence Ltd.

BTS 52

THE LAST POETS:
AT LAST

AT LAST
AT LAST
AT LAST
AT LAST
AT LAST
AT LAST
AT LAST
AT LAST
AT LAST
AT LAST
AT LAST
AT LAST
AT LAST
AT LAST
AT LAST
AT LAST

AT LAST
AT LAST
AT LAST
AT LAST
AT LAST
AT LAST
AT LAST
AT LAST
AT LAST
AT LAST
AT LAST
AT LAST
AT LAST
AT LAST
AT LAST
AT LAST

POETS:
SULIAMAN EL-HADI
UMAR BIN-HASSEN
JALAL-UDDIN MANSUR
NURIDDIN

MUSICIANS:
TENOR SAX • BROTHER JUICE
ALTO SAX • CLAUDE LAWRENCE
PIANO • CASA BURAK
DRUMS • PHILIP KING
BASS • DUKE CLEAMONS

THE LAST POETS At Last **Blue Thumb Records** 1973
Design by Sundiata Keita **Photography by** Edmund (Majur) Watkins

SOL Sol **GCP** 1975

CREATIVE ARTS ENSEMBLE New Horizons **Riza Records** 1983
Cover Artwork by Napthali

IMPULSE RECORDS IN THE 1970S

Impulse! Records established its reputation with a stunning set of albums recorded by John Coltrane between 1962 and 1967. Coltrane also brought other artists into the label, effectively acting as Impulse! Records' unofficial A&R: Archie Shepp, McCoy Tyner, Elvin Jones, Alice Coltrane, Pharoah Sanders and others.

Coltrane's albums and those in his wake were serious business; not only were they the vanguard of the avant-garde, free and new jazz movements but their records also sold. As earlier noted, Coltrane's 'A Love Supreme' sold over 100,000 when it came out and is, today, one of the bestselling jazz albums of all time.

When Coltrane died from liver cancer at the age of 40 on 17 July 1967, the expectation may have been that that the house he helped build would collapse. All Coltrane's albums for Impulse! were produced by Bob Thiele, who wisely knew to take a back seat creatively, leaving the musicians in the studio to be guided by Coltrane alone. Thiele also let Coltrane use the studio whenever the spirit took him.

This proved fortuitous – Coltrane had recorded sessions faster than Impulse! could release them, and a further dozen or so unreleased albums were released posthumously throughout the 1970s. This tape digging continues to this day. Impulse! most recently released 'Both Directions at Once: The Lost Album' in 2018, and 'Blue World', a previously unreleased soundtrack to 'Le Chat Dans Le Saca', a 1964 Canadian film, in 2019.

A second departure from the label was producer Bob Thiele. He left shortly after a disagreement with Larry Newton, his new boss at parent company ABC Records over the recording of Louis Armstrong's 'What a Wonderful World'. Thiele had co-written the song (using the pseudonym George Douglas) with George Weiss. Thiele had also produced the session for Armstrong. Newton disliked the song and refused to promote it in the USA. To make matters worse, it made number one in the UK. The fallout was that Thiele left to set up a new label, Flying Dutchman.

With two key figures gone Impulse! was left in a precarious position. At the start of the 1970s, shortly after the departure of Thiele, ABC merged with Dunhill Records and Impulse! moved its offices to the West Coast of America.

Producer Ed Michel started in the music industry in the late-1950s working as a sleeve note writer for Pacific Jazz. He went on to work with Norman Granz at Verve followed by Orrin Keepnews at Riverside, where he first learnt his production skills working with artists such as Charlie Byrd.

He approached ABC, hearing that Thiele had left, and was first given the role of producing blues on their Bluesway subsidiary, working on albums by BB King and John Lee Hooker before moving to Impulse!. Michel knew he wanted the artists themselves to control the feel of record sessions but was still surprised when Pharoah Sanders would turn up for a recording with an entourage of dancers, singers and even cooks. Nevertheless, Michel recorded all the members of Coltrane's family of artists at Impulse! still under contract with the label – Pharoah Sanders, Alice Coltrane, Archie Shepp, et al – with a musical and creative empathy few could have hoped for.

He travelled to Alice Coltrane's home to record 'Ptah El Daoud' in her basement in Dix Hills, New York in September 1970. As well as producing Alice Coltrane, Michel curated the remaining tapes of John Coltrane alongside her, resulting in new Coltrane albums such as 'Live in Seattle' (1971), and 'Interstellar Space' (1974).

Michel was also instrumental in arranging for Sun Ra's Saturn Records catalogue to be released through Impulse! and through the first half of the 1970s a steady stream of high-quality Ra albums were released, mastered from the original tapes and complete with striking new sleeve designs. Albums such as 'Magic City' (1973), 'The Nubians of Plutonia' (1974) and 'Angels and Demons at play' (1974), helped to bring Sun Ra's music to a wider audience.

Through Michel's involvement and its artists roster, Impulse! remained, in the 1970s, a vitally important jazz label, major or otherwise, releasing unparalleled high-quality spiritual jazz music. Sad to say that a change at ABC's management and a change in focus towards rock music meant that Michel was unceremoniously fired in 1974. Alice Coltrane and Pharoah Sanders' contracts ended and were not renewed, and highly-credible artists moved away to other labels. Michel moved to Horizon Records. Esmond Edwards was brought in to Impulse! as producer, but new recordings reduced dramatically. In 1979 the label was sold to MCA and lay dormant until the next millennium when it was revived by Universal Music.

PHAROAH SANDERS Karma **Impulse!** 1969
Design by Barbara & Robert Flynn **Photography by** Chuck Stewart

ALBERT AYLER Love Cry **Impulse!** 1968
Design by Barbara & Robert Flynn **Photography by** Chuck Stewart

ARCHIE SHEPP The Way Ahead **Impulse!** 1968
Cover by Robert & Barbara Flynn

MARION BROWN Sweet Earth Flying **Impulse!** 1974
Photography by Michael W. Anderson **Design by** Tim Bryant

ALICE COLTRANE Lord of Lords **Impulse!** 1972

MARION BROWN Geechee Recollections **Impulse!** 1973
Photography by Donald M. Shaw

SUN RA Atlantis **Impulse!** 1973
Design by Ruby Mazur **Cover Artwork by** Alan Sekuler

MICHAEL WHITE Spirit Dance **Impulse!** 1972
Design by Philip Melnick **Photography by** Ed Michel and Philip Melnick

ALICE COLTRANE Huntington Ashram Monastery **Impulse!** 1969
Photography by Chuck Stewart **Design by** George Whiteman

SUN RA Angels And Demons At Play **Impulse!** 1974 (Originally issued on El Saturn Records, 1967)
Illustration by Cathy Endfield **Design by** Tim Bryant

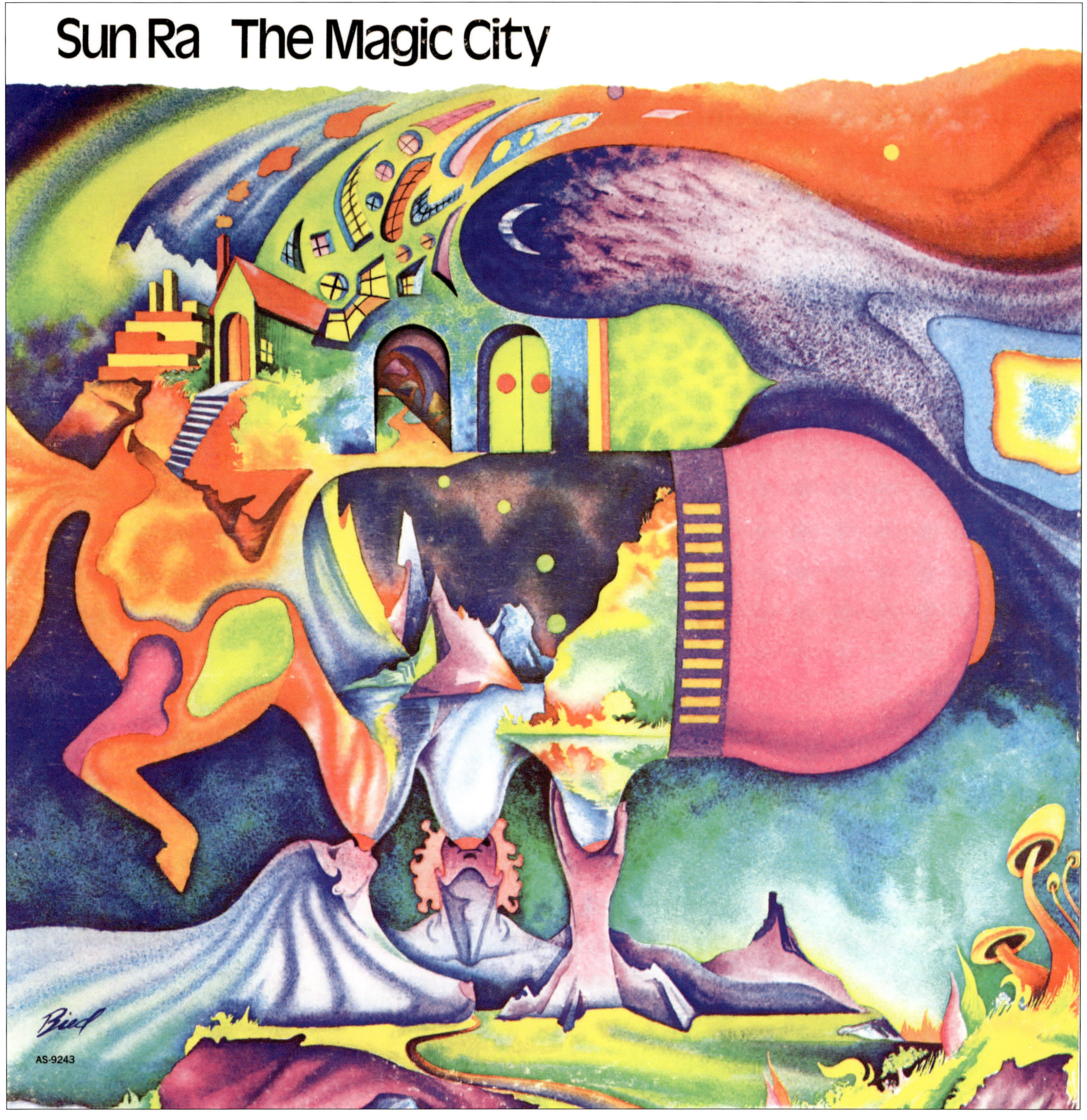

SUN RA Angels And Demons At Play **Impulse!** 1974 (Originally issued on El Saturn Records, 1967)
Illustration by Cathy Endfield **Design by** Tim Bryant

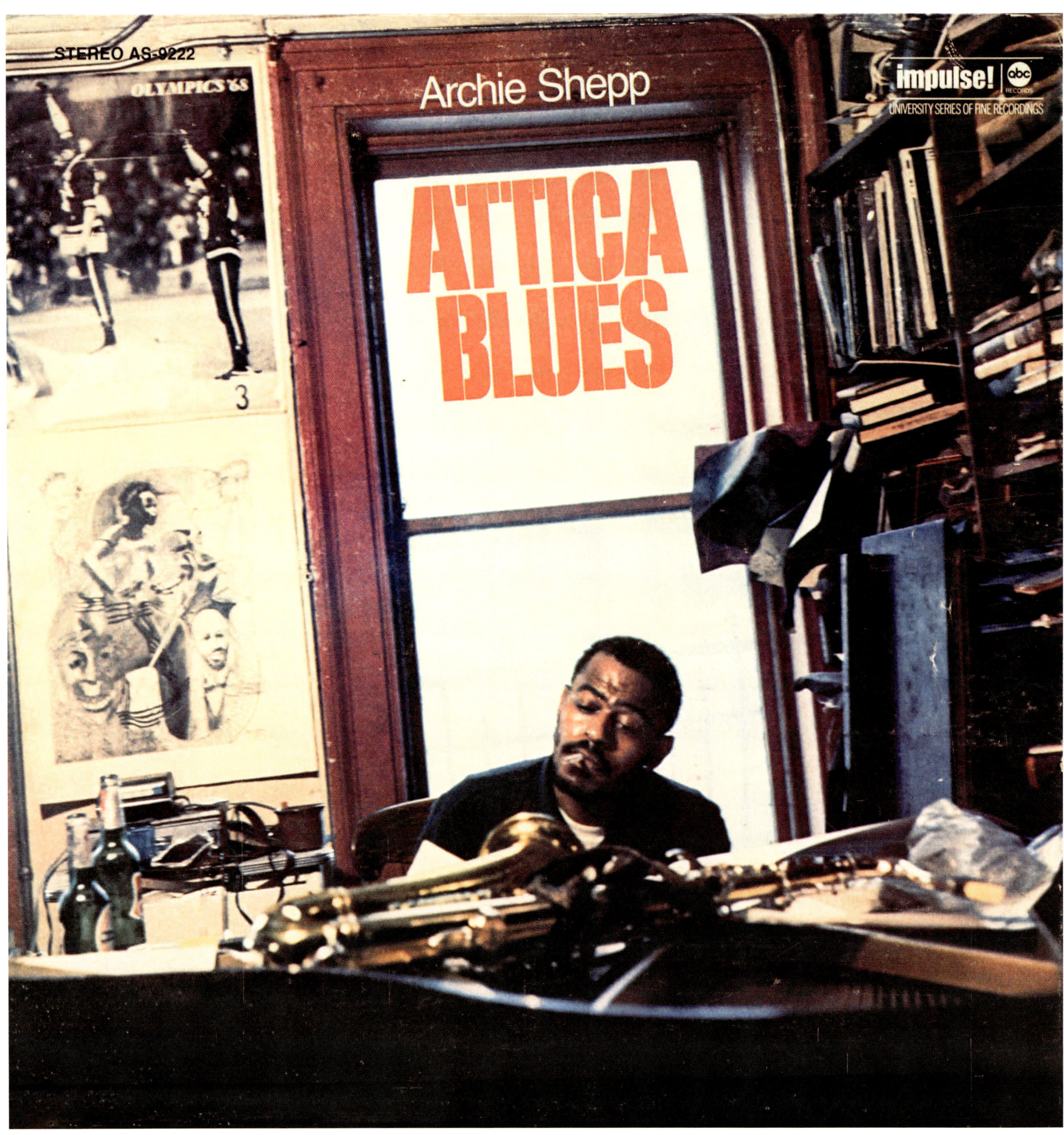

ARCHIE SHEPP Attica Blues **Impulse!** 1972
Photography by Chuck Stewart **Design by** Clyde Gilliam

JOHN COLTRANE Selflessness Featuring My Favourite Things **Impulse!** 1968

SUN RA Fate In A Pleasant Mood **Impulse!** 1974
Illustration by Bodhi Wind **Design by** Tim Bryant

ARCHIE SHEPP Things Have Got To Change **Impulse!** 1971
Design by Wallace Caldwell-Porter **Photography by** Chuck Stewart

ALICE COLTRANE WITH STRINGS World Galaxy **Impulse!** 1972
Cover & Design Peter Max **Photography by** Philip Melnick

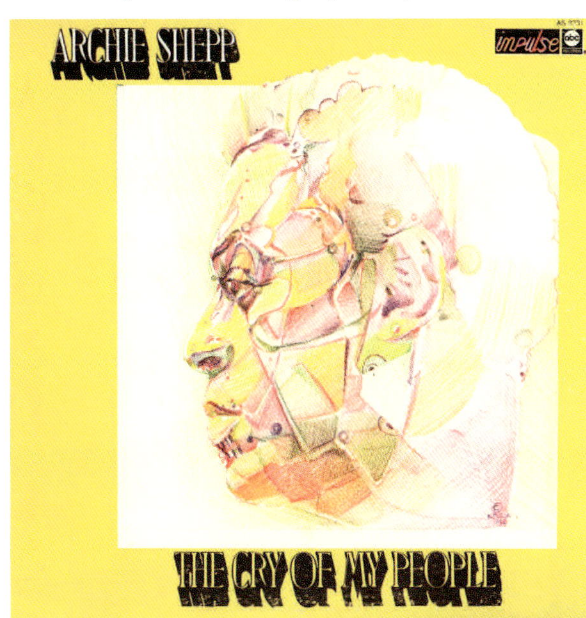

ARCHIE SHEPP The Cry Of My People **Impulse!** 1973
Illustration by Nelson Stevens **Design by** Ruby Mazur

YUSEF LATEEF Psychicemotus **Impulse!** 1966
Design by Robert Flynn **Photography by** Chuck Stewart

ALICE COLTRANE Universal Consciousness **Impulse!** 1971
Design and Photography by Philip Melnick

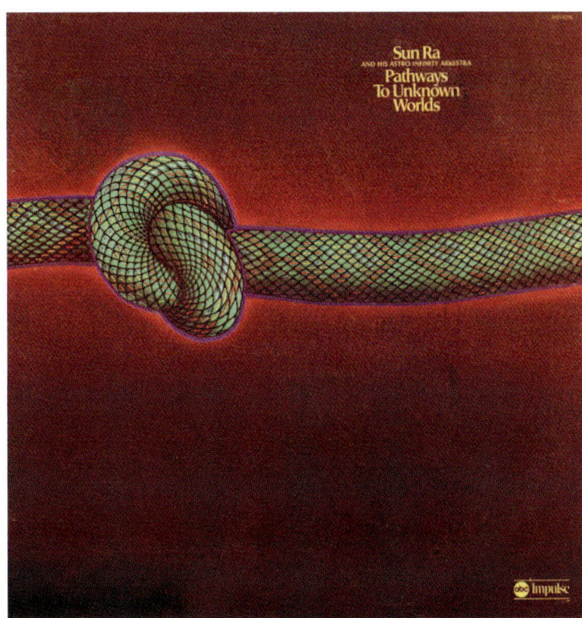

SUN RA AND HIS ASTRO INFINITY ARKESTRA Pathways To Unknown Worlds **Impulse!** 1975 **Design** Earl Klasky & Martin Donald
Photography by Jim McCrary

ALBERT AYLER The Last Album **Impulse!** 1971
Design by Woody Woodward Grafix **Illustration by** Lorel Michel

ART ENSEMBLE OF CHICAGO The Spiritual **Freedom** / **Polydor** 1972
Design by Hamish Grimes **Graphics by** Phillip Gotlop **Photography by** Jan Persson

GARY BARTZ NTU TROOP Home! **Milestone** 1970
Design by John Murello **Photography by** Robert O. Torrence

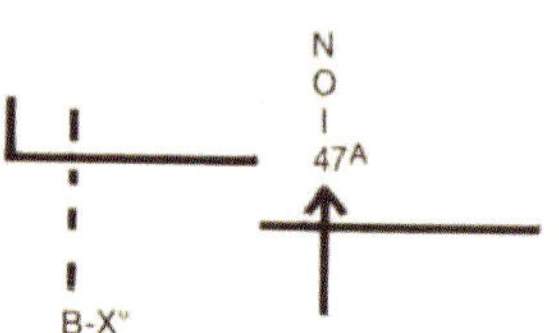

ANTHONY BRAXTON B-XO NO-47A **Actual/BYG Records** 1969
Photography by Philippe Gras & Jacques Bisceglia

BABATUNDE
AND PHENOMENA

LEVELS OF
CONCIOUSNESS

BABATUNDE AND PHENOMENA Levels of Consciousness **Theresa Records** 1979
Art Direction and Photography by James McCaffry

ART
ENSEMBLE
OF
CHICAGO

(AACM)

people in sorrow

ART ENSEMBLE OF CHICAGO (AACM) People In Sorrow **Odeon Japan** 1969 (Originally issued on Pathé, France 1969)
Photography by Horace

FRED TOMPKINS Somesville **F.K.T. Records** 1975

HAMIET BLUIETT QUARTET We Have Come To Save You From Yourselves **India Navigation** 1979 **Design by** Hamiet Bluiett

CHARLES TYLER Live In Europe: Jazz Festival **UMEA AK-BA Records** 1977 **Design by** Kathleen Tyler

STEVE LACY Stamps **Hat Hut Records** 1979 **Cover Art by** Klaus Baumgärtner

JOE McPHEE Rotation **Hat Hut Records** 1977 **Cover Art by** Klaus-Baumgärtner
s

STANTON DAVIS Manhattan Melody **Enja** 1988 **Cover Artwork by** Gerhard Ehrmann

HAMIET BLUIETT Endangered Species **India Navigation** 1976 **Cover Artwork by** Bob Younger **Photography by** Jacki Ochs

THE GAP MANGIONE Diana In The Autumn Wind **GRC** 1968

MUSIC INC / CHARLES TOLIVER The Ringer **Polydor** 1969 **Photography by** Val Wilmer

STANLEY COWELL Blues For The Viet Cong **Polydor** 1969

The Unpredictability of Predictability

JEROME COOPER

JEROME COOPER The Unpredictability of Predictability **About Time Records** 1979
Design by Therese Bolton **Photography by** Doug Fidoten

MARY LOU WILLIAMS Live At The Cookery **Chiaroscuro Records** 1976
Cover and Design by John Devries

GARY BARTZ NTU TROOP Follow the Medicine Man **Prestige** 1973
Cover Artwork by Ron Warwell

REGGIE S Give Me Back Some Lovin' **Shasa Records** 1983

PAT-1062

ALL ALONE

MAL
WALDRON
LIVE
2

MAL WALDRON All Alone Mal Waldron Live 2 **Fontana** 1974
Design by Heyqlow Kobayashi

PRINCE LAWSHA Firebirds Live At Berkeley Jazz Festival Vol I **Birdseye** 1976
Art Direction by Mary Lawsha **Design by** Padreigin McGillicuddy

FULL CIRCLE s/t **Bean Records** 1977

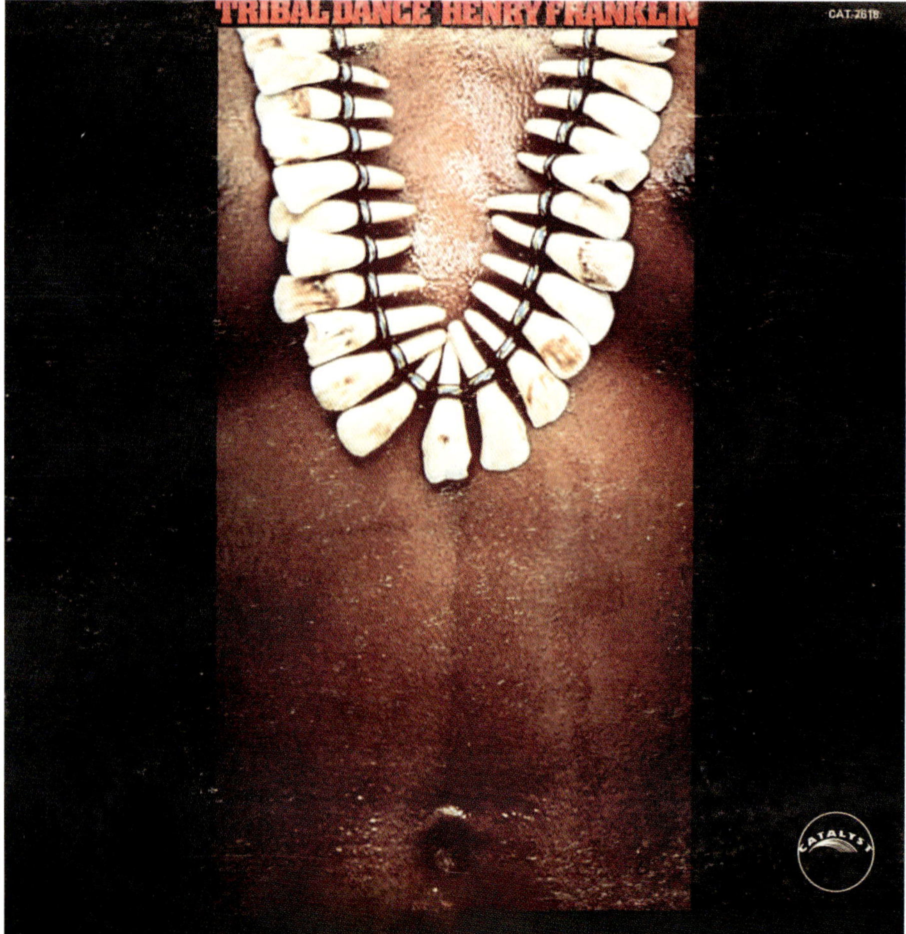

HENRY FRANKLIN Tribal Dance **Catalyst Records** 1977
Art Direction by David Lartaud **Photography by** Jim Cummins

DEWEY REDMAN The Ear Of The Behearer **Impulse!** 1973

BYARD LANCASTER Exodus **Philly Jazz** 1977
Cover Painting by Tony Dunham

MAL WALDRON Moods **Enja Records 1978**
Design by Winckelmann and Weber **Photography by** Gert Chesi

GATO BARBIERI & DON CHERRY Togetherness **Durium** 1974 (Original Durium 1966)

MARC LEVIN The Dragon Suite **Savoy Records** 1968
Painting by Joseph Westerfield **Photography by** Charles Gatewood

GT/SLP–100

Free Angela

sung by LARRY SAUNDERS The Prophet of Soul

Available Through
THE NATIONAL UNITED COMMITTEE TO FREE ANGELA DAVIS
2085 SUTTER STREET, SAN FRANCISCO, CAL. 94115
NEW YORK COMMITTEE TO FREE ANGELA DAVIS
150 5th AVENUE, NEW YORK, NEW YORK 10011

LARRY SAUNDERS Free Angela **Golden Triangle Records** 1971

ETHEL ENNIS Live At The Maryland **INN EnE Productions** 1980

COUNTRY GIRL

AMINA CLAUDINE MYERS SEXTET

AMINA CLAUDINE MYERS SEXTET Country Girl **Minor Music** 1986
Design by Christin Schindler & Claus Peter Bäuerle **Photography by** Mark LeBon

THE CREATOR'S MUSICIAN

ROBERTO MIGUEL MIRANDA

ROBERTO MIGUEL MIRANDA The Creator's Musician **Nimbus West Records** 1980

DICK CROOK

OPEN DOORS

DICK CROOK Open Doors **Polar Bear Records** 1982
Design by Richard Dworkin **Photography by** Don Nguyen

Fantasy Island

MORRIS WILSON Fantasy Island **MoWil Records** 1981
Photography by Greg Helgeson

DON CHERRY Brown Rice **EMI** 1975
Cover by Moki Cherry

Om Mani Padme Hum
DON
BROWN RICE
ORGANIC MUSIC

SEDITION ENSEMBLE Regeneration Report **Context Music** 1981

LLOYD McNEILL / MARSHALL HAWKINS Tanner Suite **ASHA** 1969
Design by Lloyd McNeill

MARY LOU WILLIAMS TRIO Zodiac Suite **Folkway Records** 1975

SUN RA AND HIS ARKESTRA Bad & Beautiful **Impulse!** 1975 5 (Originally released on El Saturn label 1972)
Design by Tim Bryant **Photography by** Jim McCrary

ROOTS OF THE REVOLUTION

While Miles Davis, John Coltrane and Ornette Coleman signalled the arrival of a new jazz movement after bebop, other equally ground-breaking artists also played their part in its evolution.

Although Art Blakey is primarily associated with hard bop, he was also instrumental in bringing African and Latin rhythms to jazz music, which would prove to be a key factor in the evolution of a more Afro-centric jazz that emerged in the 1960s.

In 1947, Blakey went to Africa for three months and ended up staying for two years. Initially he went to study religion and philosophy, and during this period converted to Islam, taking the name Abdullah Ibn Buhaina. On his return to New York, his band The Jazz Messengers became a school for future stars of modern jazz through the 1960s and onwards and included players such as Lee Morgan, Benny Golson, Wayne Shorter, Freddie Hubbard, Bobby Timmons and Curtis Fuller. 'Holiday for Skins' (Pts. I and II) were released by Blue Note Records in 1958, featuring Latin percussionists Sabu Martinez, Ray Barretto, Julio Martinez and Chonguito Vincente. The music was a pioneering riot of stripped back African and Latin rhythms, chants and jazz. Other releases by Blakey such as 'Drum Suite' (1957), (featuring statues of African deities on the cover), Ritual (1957) and African Beat (1962) similarly showed Blakey to be a leading figure in connecting jazz music to its African roots.

Another important artist to incorporate African elements into his early music was Randy Weston. The large-scale suite 'Uhuru Afrika' (1960), a historic landmark album, that included the participation of poet Langston Hughes, celebrated the independence of a number of new African countries. Weston visited Lagos, Nigeria, in 1961 as part of a US cultural exchange program sponsored by the American Society of African Culture in a contingent which included Langston Hughes, Lionel Hampton, Ahmed Abdul-Malik, Nina Simone and Brock Peters. On his return he composed the album 'Highlife: Music from the New African Nations featuring the Highlife' (1963).

Yusef Lateef must be credited with bringing Middle Eastern and Asian music, instrumentation and philosophical ideas into the realm of jazz, foreseeing the arrival of 'world music' by at least two decades. Lateef began his career as a solo artist at Savoy Records in 1957 releasing 'Prayer to the East' the same year. By the time of 'Eastern Sounds', recorded for Prestige in 1962, Lateef was experimenting with exotic instrumentation such as rahab, shanai, arghul, koto, Chinese wooden flutes and bells alongside his flute and saxophone, and employing 'eastern' scales and modes in his music. Lateef drew the attention of Bob Thiele and, in 1964,he signed with Impulse! Records alongside John Coltrane, McCoy Tyner, Max Roach, Archie Shepp and Elvin Jones.

MAX ROACH We Insist! Freedom Now Suite **Candid Records** 1961
Photography Hugh Bell & Paul Bacon

THE JAZZ MESSENGERS FEATURING ART BLAKEY Ritual Swing **Des Disques Pacific Jazz Records** 1957
Cover Artwork by John Altoon **Design by** William Caxton **Photography by** Lee Friedlander

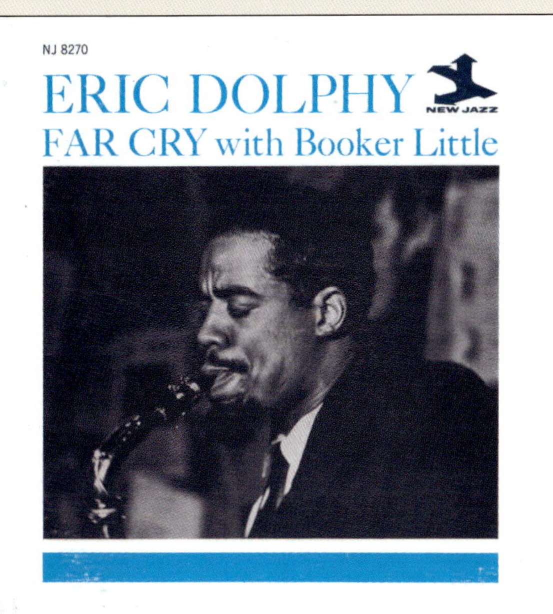

ERIC DOLPHY Far Cry **New Jazz Records** 1962

ABBEY LINCOLN Abbey Is Blue **Riverside Records** 1959
Cover Artwork Lewine, Braren, Bacon **Photography** Lawrence N. Shustak

AHMAD JAMAL Chamber Music Of The New Jazz **Argo Records** 1956

YUSEF LATEEF AND HIS MEN Jazz For The Thinker
Savoy Records 1957

DIZZY GILLESPIE Afro **Columbia Records** 1956

MILES DAVIS Kind Of Blue **Colombia Records** 1959

A.K. SALIM Flute Suite **Savoy Records** 1957

JOHN COLTRANE Giant Steps **Atlantic Records** 1960
Cover Artwork by Marvin Israel **Photography by** Lee Friedlander

DAVE BURNS Dave Burns **Vanguard Records** 1962
Cover Artwork by Jules Halfant **Photography by** Dave Gar

He remained there until moving over to Atlantic Records in 1967. Lateef brought an unparalleled sense of spirituality and experimentation to his body of work. Lateef was also a writer, academic and educator. Starting in 1971, he taught courses in 'autophysiopsychic music' at the Manhattan School of Music. He wrote a dissertation on the comparative study of Western and Islamic education at the University of Massachusetts Amherst, and became a researcher at the Center for Nigerian Cultural Studies at Ahmadu Bello University, Nigeria throughout the early 1980s.

Composer, pianist and theorist George Russell began his career as a drummer. In 1945 he turned down playing drums in Charlie Parker's band after developing tuberculosis. During this time he began to develop what was to become his 'Lydian Chromatic Concept of Tonal Organization', which was published in book form in 1953. Essentially Russell put forward the idea that all music is based on the tonal gravity of the Lydian mode (as opposed to the traditional notion of the Ionian mode as the centre). This idea opened up the pathway for musicians to explore modality. John Coltrane explored this Lydian concept on his ground-breaking 'Giant Steps' (1960), and Miles Davis and Bill Evans explored the notion of modality to great effect on Davis' equally portentous 'Kind of Blue'.

Max Roach and Abbey Lincoln were at the forefront of the union of jazz music with the emergence of the Civil Rights Movement. The era-defining album 'We Insist. Max Roach's Freedom Now Suite' (1961), with its startling front cover image of three men seated in protest at a segregated restaurant, was matched only by the strength of the music inside. The text on the back, written by A Philip Randolph, American labour unionist and civil rights activist read:

'A revolution is unfurling – America's unfinished revolution. It is unfurling in lunch counters, buses, libraries and schools - wherever the dignity and potential of men are denied. Youth and idealism are unfurling. Masses of Negroes are marching onto the stage of history and demanding their freedom now!'

Songs on the album included 'Freedom Day', 'Triptych: Prayer, Protest, Peace', 'All Africa' and 'Tears For Johannesburg'. The album includes Olatunji on percussion and Abbey Lincoln on vocals. It features collective improvisation, heavy percussion, as well as searing screaming vocals of pain on 'Protest'. The album was created in response to the Greensboro sit-ins at a lunch counter in Greensboro, North Carolina, and the growing momentum of the Civil Rights Movement. Max Roach wrote about the album in Downbeat magazine stating:

'We American jazz musicians of African descent have proved beyond all doubt that we're master musicians of our instruments. Now what we have to do is employ our skill to tell the dramatic story of our people and what we've been through'.

GEORGE RUSSELL Jazz **RCA Victor Records** 1957

LANGSTON HUGHES AND RANDY WESTON Afro-Percussion **Uhuru Africa (Freedom Africa) Roulette Records** 1961 **Cover Artwork by** Arnold Meyers **Photography by** Arnold Meyers

GEORGE RUSSELL SEXTET Stratusphunk **Riverside Records** 1961
Cover Artwork by Ken Deardoff **Photography by** Lawrence N. Shustak

DUKE ELLINGTON AND HIS ORCHESTRA Liberian Suite and A Tone Parallel to Harlem **Columbia Records 1956**

JULIAN PRIESTER SEXTET Spiritville **Jazzland Records** 1960

YUSEF LATEEF Lateef at Cranbrook **Argo Records** 1958
Cover Artwork by W.Hopkins

LENNY McBROWNE AND THE FOUR SOULS Eastern Lights **Riverside Records** 1960 **Cover Artwork by** Ken Deardoff **Photography by** William Claxton

WALT DICKERSON This is Walt Dickerson!
Prestige New Jazz Records 1961

KEN McINTYRE Way, Way Out **United Artists Records** 1963
Cover Arwork byt Norman Art Studio

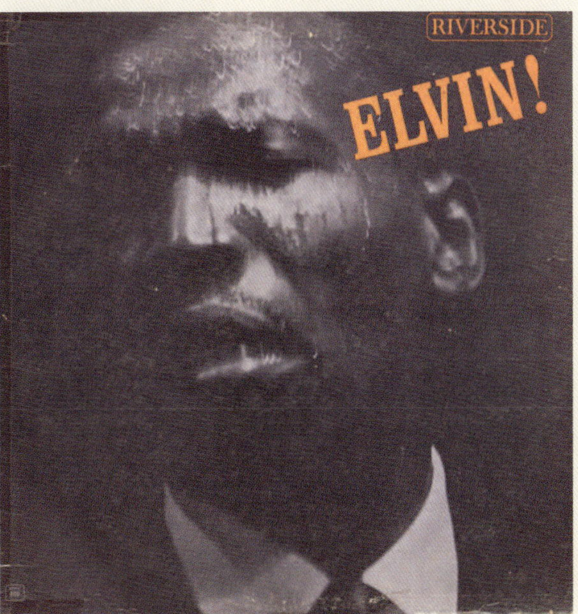

ELVIN JONES Elvin! **Riverside Records** 1962
Cover Artwork by Ken Deardoff **Photograph by** Steve Schapiro

YUSEF LATEEF Prayer To The East **Savoy Records 1957**
Design by Levy A Agency

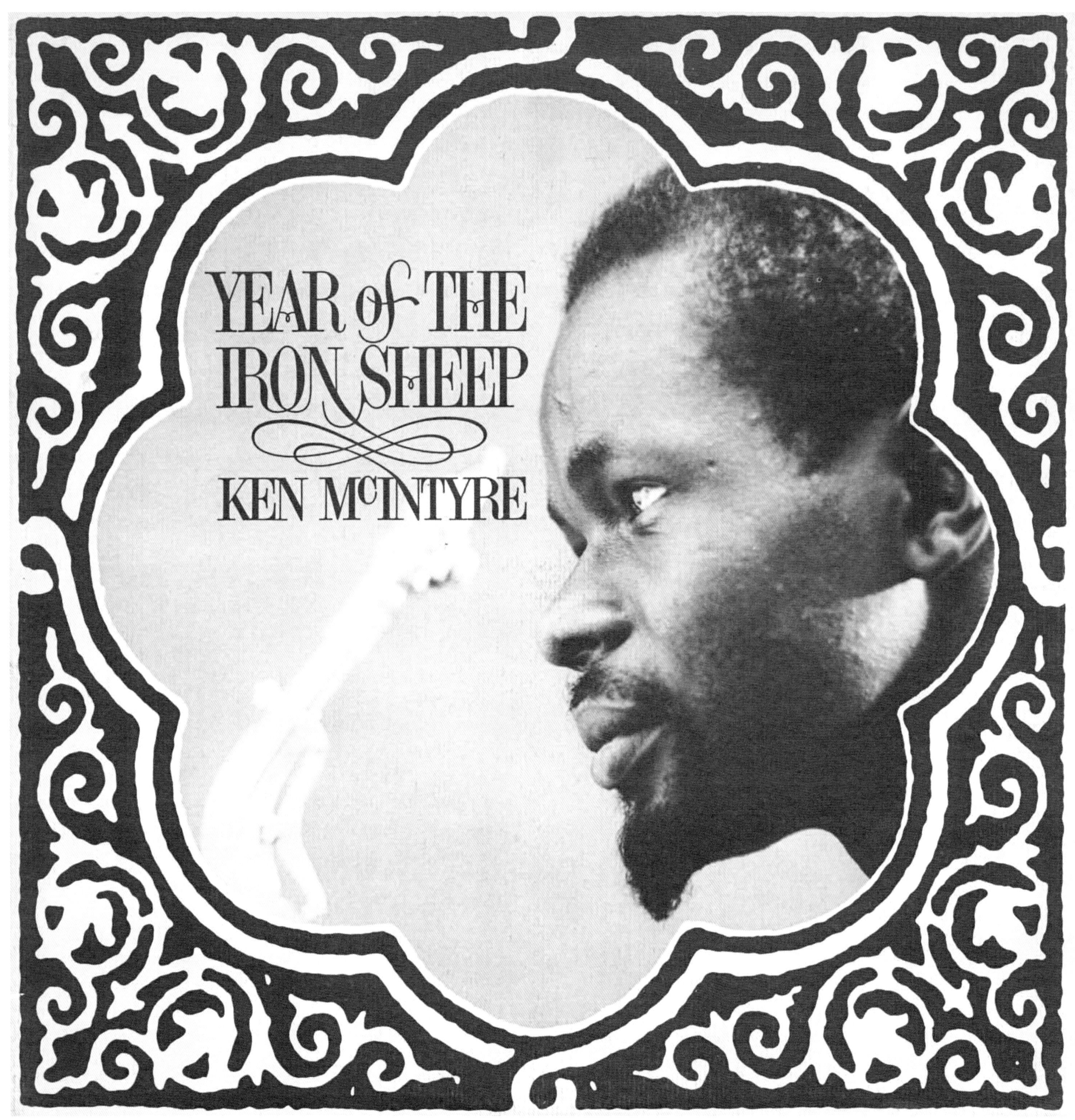

KEN McINTYRE Year Of The Iron Sheep **United Artists Jazz** 1965
Photography by Chuck Stewart

RASHIED ALI QUINTET Rashied Ali Quintet **Survival Records** 1973
Design by Mel Kirsch **Photography by** Ray Ross

PLUNKY AND ONENESS OF JUJU Every Way But Loose **Sutra** 1982 (Original 'Make a Change' Black Fire 1980)
Design by Denny M. Williams **Photography by** Lew Harrison

DON CHERRY Eternal Rhythm **MPS Records** 1972 (Original 1969)
Design by Heinz Bähr **Photography by** Hans Harzheim & Josef Werkmeister

FLYING DUTCHMAN

Flying Dutchman was created by Bob Thiele following his departure from Impulse! Records in 1969. As John Coltrane's producer, Thiele had more kudos than pretty much anyone alive in the music business and was able to draw upon this in establishing the label.

Set up primarily as a jazz label, Thiele was determined to tap into the spirit of the times with Flying Dutchman, releasing a startling mixture of forward-thinking jazz, radical black politics, experimental music and more.

He released powerful speeches by Black Panther spokesperson H Rap Brown, Marxist, feminist activist Angela Davis and anti-Vietnam poetry (Peter Hamill's 'Massacre at My Lai'). The label also released pioneering electro-acoustic experimental releases by composer Jon Appleton (including 'Human Music', an album with Don Cherry) and others.

But it was in the area of spiritual jazz that Flying Dutchman came into full bloom with pioneering works by radical artists: Ornette Coleman ('Friends and Neighbors' (1970) recorded live at Coleman's new live/work space on Prince Street, New York); the first release by Horace Tapscott ('The Giant Is Awakened' (1969)); George Russell presents The Esoteric Circle (recorded in Norway in 1969, featuring Jan Garbarek, Terje Rypdal, Arild Andersen and Jon Christensen) and others. Soon a number of major figures emerged on the label - Gil Scott-Heron, Lonnie Liston Smith, Leon Thomas and Gato Barbieri.

Flying Dutchman's last great year was 1975 with the release of Liston Smith's 'Expansions' as well as releases by Gato Barbieri, Richard Groove Holmes and Oliver Nelson, but by 1978 the label had closed. In 1983, Thiele emerged once more with a new label Doctor Jazz and then another, Red Baron Records, which he ran from 1991 up until his death in 1996. Flying Dutchman was relaunched in 2020 by Thiele's son, Bob Thiele Jr with the catalogue re-released by Ace Records.

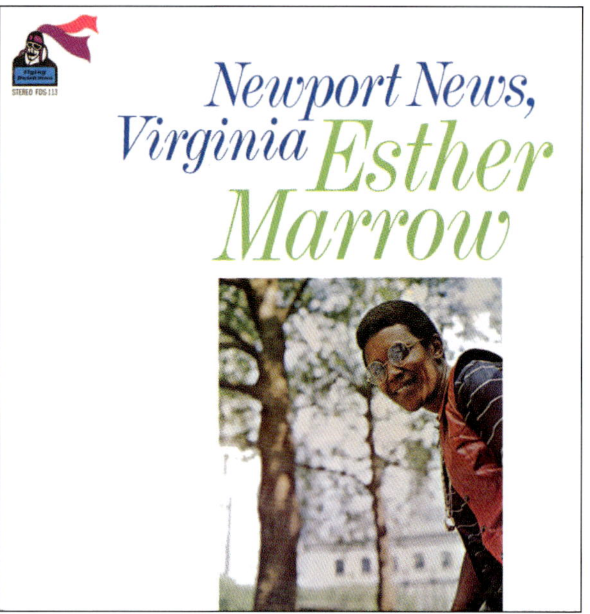

ESTHER MARROW Newport News, Virginia **Flying Dutchman** 1970 **Photography by** Irv Glaser **Design by** Robert Flynn

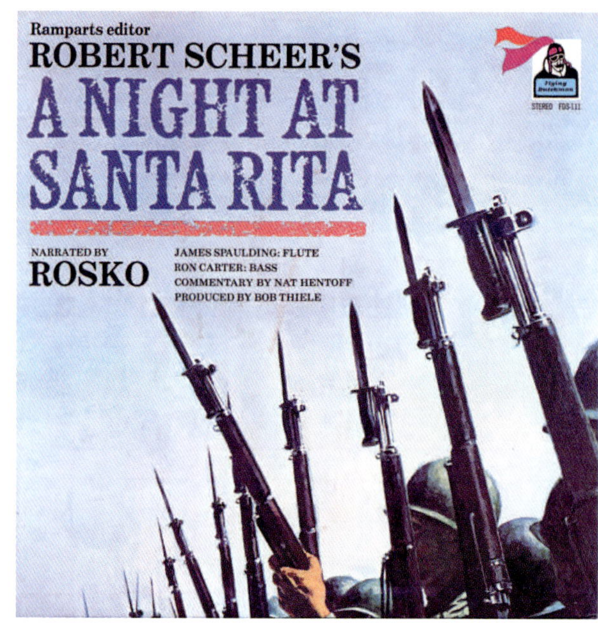

ROBERT SCHEER'S A Night At Santa Rita **Flying Dutchman** 1969 **Cover Painting by** Victor Kalin **Design By** Robert Flynn

LONNIE LISTON SMITH & THE COSMIC ECHOES Expansions **Flying Dutchman** 1975 **Artwork by** Jack (John) Martin **Art Direction by** Acy Lehman & Dick Smith

LEON THOMAS Blues And The Soulful Truth **Flying Dutchman** 1972 **Drawing by** Hideo Yamashita **Design by** Haig Adishian **Photography by** Giuseppe Pino

HAROLD ALEXANDER Sunshine Man **Flying Dutchman** 1971 **Design by** Haig Adishian **Photography by** Charles Stewart

ROSKO Pete Hamils Massacre At My Lai **Flying Dutchman** 1969 **Painting & Cover Artwork by** Victor Kalin **Design by** Robert Flynn

GIL SCOTT-HERON The Revolution Will Not Be Televised **Flying Dutchman** 1974
Photography by Charles Stewart

CHICO FREEMAN Kings of Mali **India Navigation Records** 1978
Photography by Beth Cummins

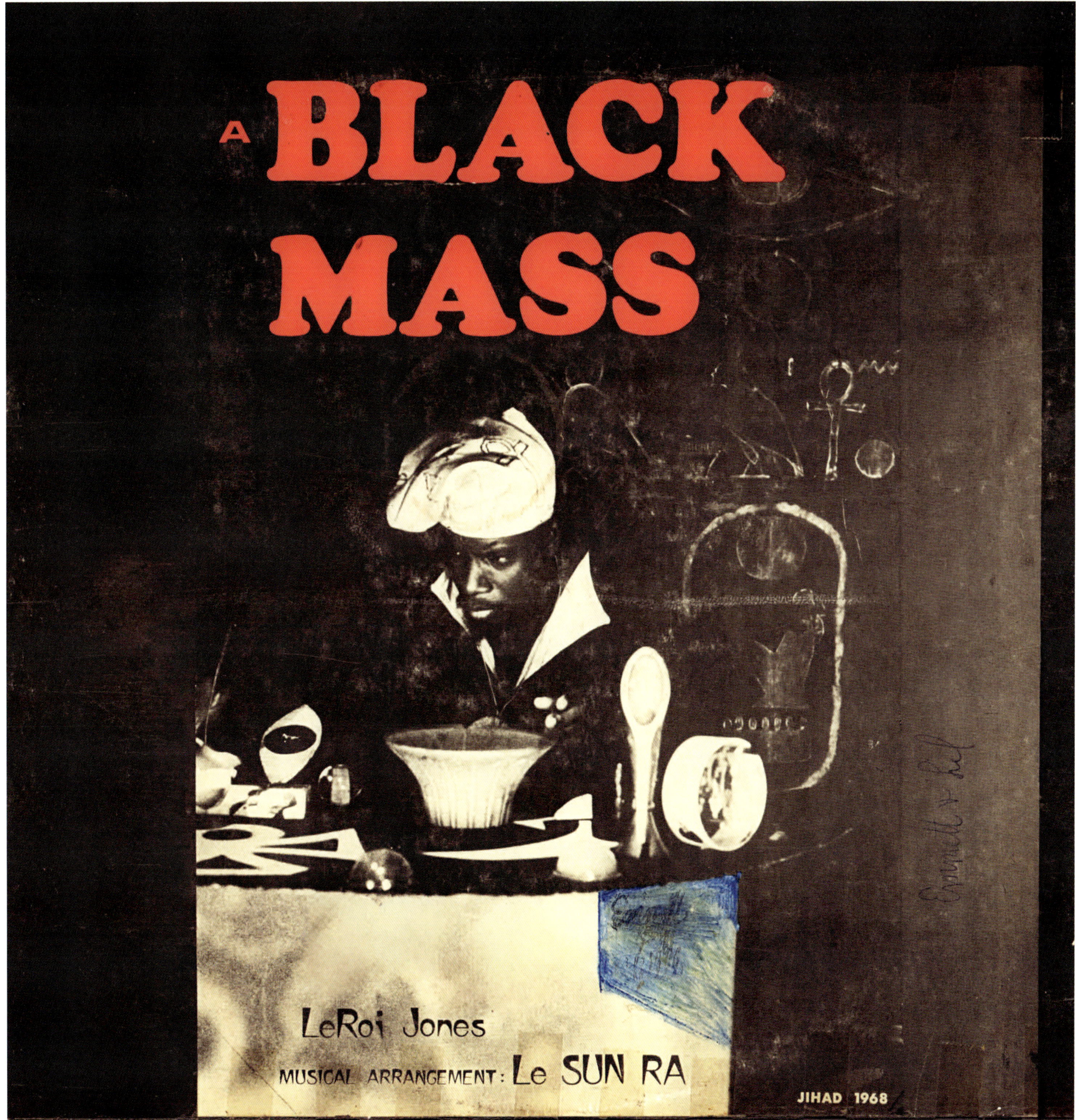

LEROI JONES (AMIRI BARAKA) AND SUN RA Black Mass **Jihad** 1968

THE LIGHTMEN As Free As You Wanna Be **Judnell** 1970
Photography by Ralph Cooper

JAZZ CONTEMPORARIES Strata-East Records 1973 Original released 1972
Design by Warren Shipp

COUSIN WASH & NDIKO THE ENVIRONMENTAL STUDIES PROJECT Presents Cousin Wash The Story Teller & Ndiko The Musician **BERCO** 1971 **Cover Artwork by** Joe Geran

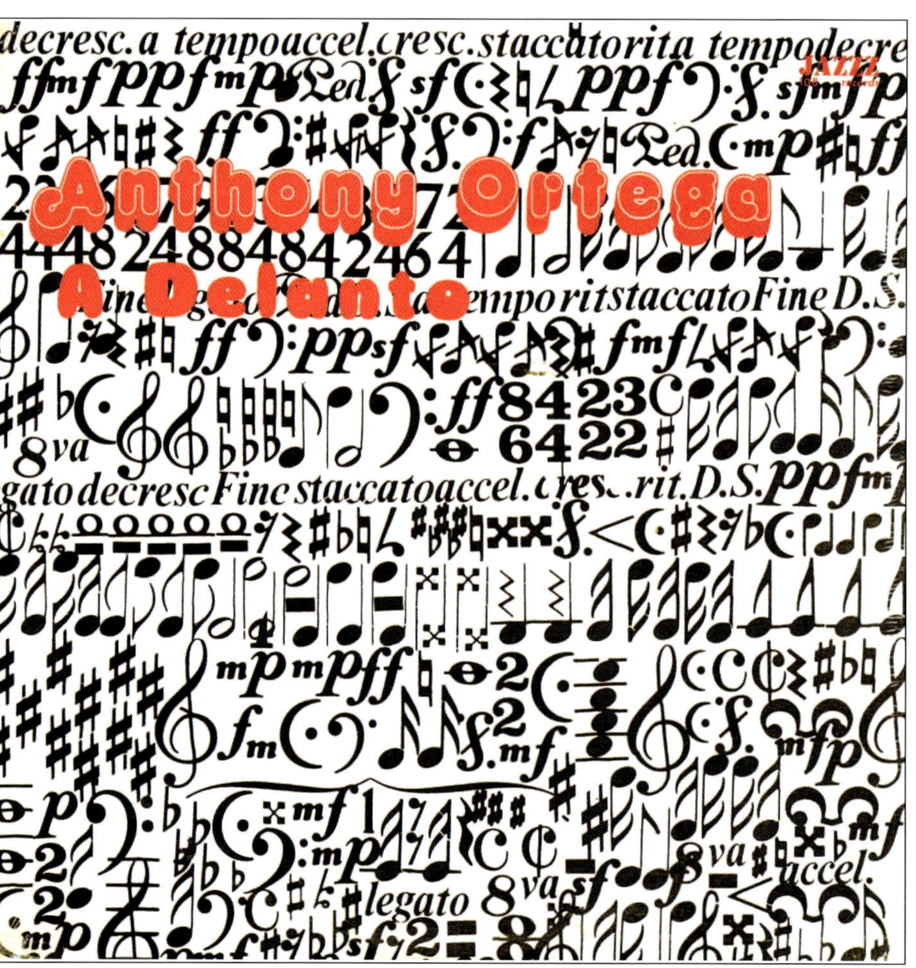

ANTHONY ORTEGA A Delanto **Jazzz Records** 1976

SUN RA Nuits De La Fondation Maeght Vol. I. **Recommended Records** 1981

DUKE ELLINGTON PRESENTS
THE DOLLAR BRAND TRIO
reprise

ANTHONY BRAXTON
SIX DUETS (1982)
featuring:
JOHN LINDBERG
CECMA 1005
STEREO

Anthony Braxton
MOERS MUSIC
Seven Compositions 1978

UNDERSTANDING
BOBBY NAUGHTON UNITS
STEREO

CJF
UNIVERSITY OF NOTRE DAME, APRIL 6 - 7, 1962

Orion
JAZZ IS NOW
THE JOHNNY FRIGO SEXTET
10 MODERN JAZZ DANCES
CHOREOGRAPHED BY GUS GIORDANO

KENYA YA AFRICA
Sadao Watanabe Meets Inter-African Theatre Group

MTUME

DEDICATION
HERBIE HANCOCK

hat
JOE McPHEE PO MUSIC:
OLEO

STEREO
Jazz of the Seventies
Sam Rivers Tuba Trio
Essence - Part X with Joe Daley & Warren Smith
live
Earl Cross Sextet with Jimmy Vass
Daoud Haroon
Ronnie Boykins
Juma Sultan
Roger Blank
J. L. March
Una Muy Bonita

Ambiance
Ebun

ELVIN JONES...TIME CAPSULE...ELVIN JONES...TIME CAPSULE
VANGUARD

Maria's First
CALVIN KEYS

ROLAND KIRK
left & right
ATLANTIC

the rubáiyát of dorothy ashby
original compositions inspired by the words of omar khayyam, arranged and conducted by richard evans

EMI
VOICES
RANDY MASTERS FEATURING SOLAR PLEXUS

STEINWAY & SONS

AUDIO FIDELITY
AFLP 2131
WALT DICKERSON plays
UNITY
A STUDY IN HIGH FIDELITY SOUND

NEW YORK ART QUARTET

Mike Nock
STRATA
Suite from film
DAYBREAK – GUARDIAN ANGEL – AURORA AUSTRALIS – AFTER SATIE – OPARARA

JOE HENDERSON
THE ELEMENTS
FEATURING ALICE COLTRANE
CHARLIE HADEN
PROMOTION-Not For Sale

firebirds
PRINCE LASHA & SONNY SIMMONS

'ROUND ABOUT MIDNIGHT
MARY LOU WILLIAMS
Vogue

MAX ROACH · LIFT EVERY VOICE AND SING
WITH THE J.C.WHITE SINGERS
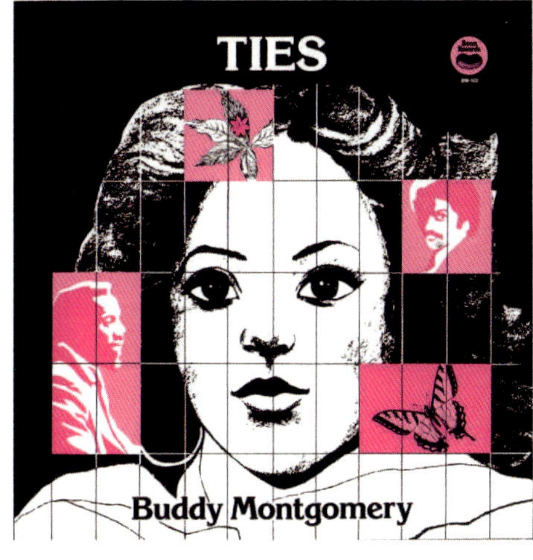
TIES
Buddy Montgomery

NEW ART JAZZ ENSEMBLE
revelation-9 stereo
SEEKING
John Carter
Bobby Bradford
Bruz Freeman
Tom Williamson

ARCHIE SHEPP · CORAL ROCK
Prestige

Gil Scott-Heron and Brian Jackson
It's Your World
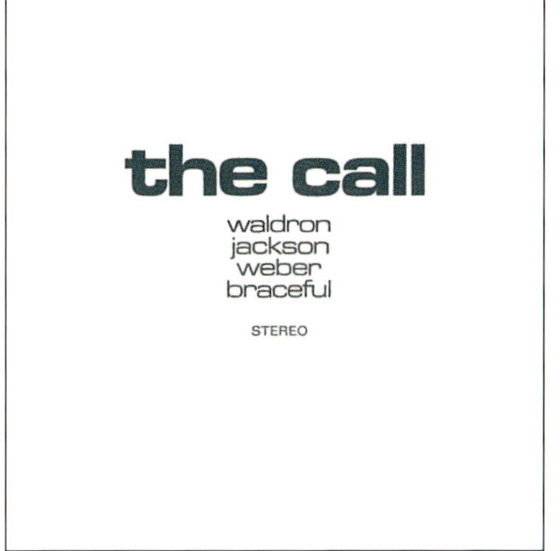
the call
waldron
jackson
weber
braceful
STEREO

Skizoke
The Frank Lowe Sextet

JAZZ SYMPHONICS The Beginning **Renfro Records** 1968

LESTER BOWIE African Children **Hero Records** 1978
Art Direction by Antonio Ortolan **Design by** Maria Teresa Tannozzini **Photography by** Isio Saba

JOHN COLTRANE Infinity **Impulse!** 1972
Design & Illustration by Richard Taylor **Photography By** Chester Sheard

IMAMU AMIRI BARAKA It's Nation Time African Visionary Music **Black Forum** 1972
Photography by Fundi

MAL WALDRON The American Festival Of Negro Arts Presents: Les Nuits De La Negritude Reflections In Modern Jazz **Powertree Records Inc** 1965
Photography By Don Greenhaus

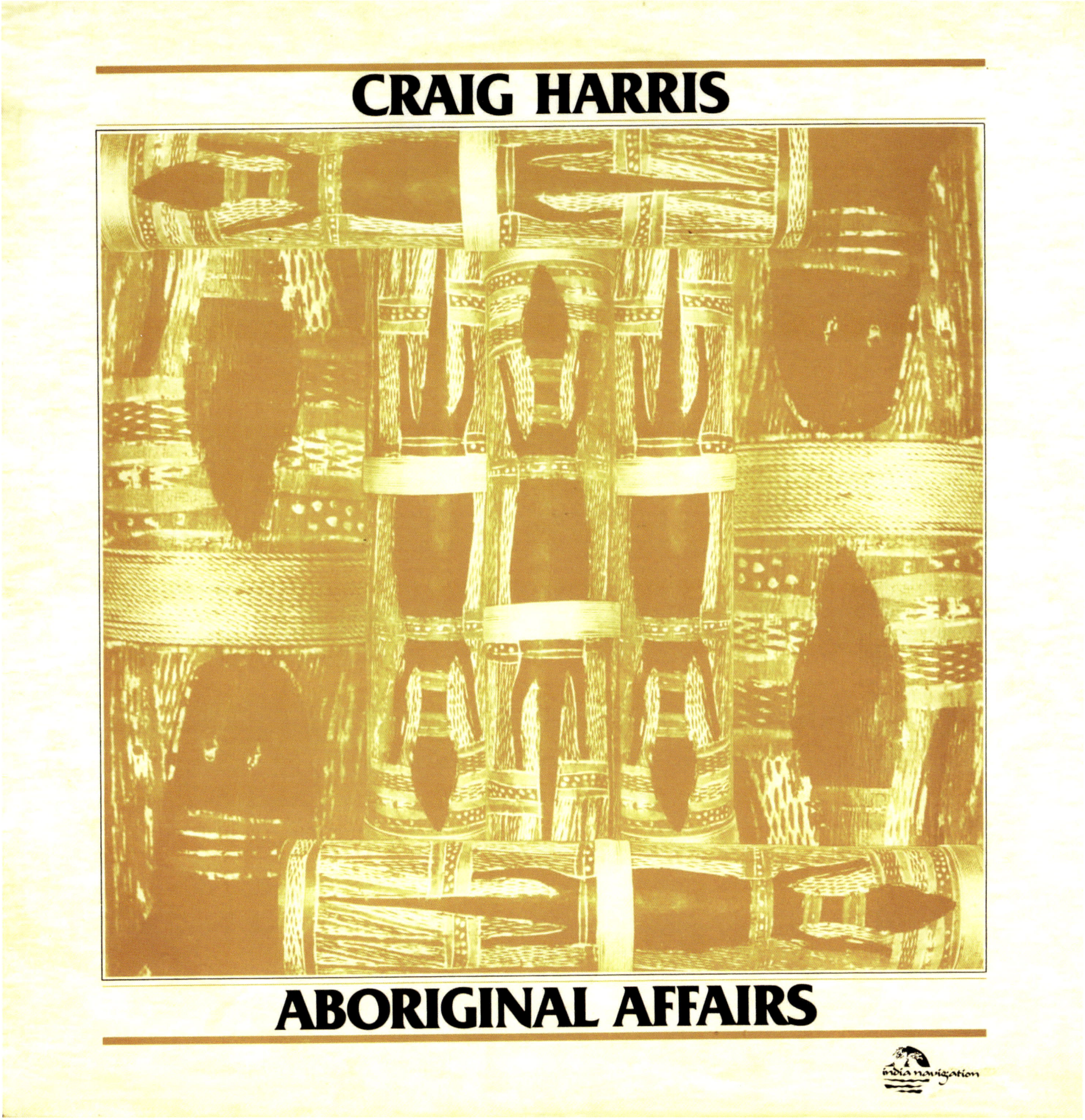

CRAIG HARRIS Aboriginal Affairs **India Navigation** 1983
Design by Koji Morioka **Photography by** Beth Cummins

RAHSAAN ROLAND KIRK Blacknuss **Atlantic Records** 1972
Cover Artwork by Haig Adishan **Photography by** Ray Ross

HAROLD LAND QUINTET The Peace-Maker **Cadet** 1968
Design & Photography by Jerry Griffith **Photography by** Fred Seligo

PRINCE BILLY MAHDI WRIGHT You Got Dat Wright **Raenii** 1982

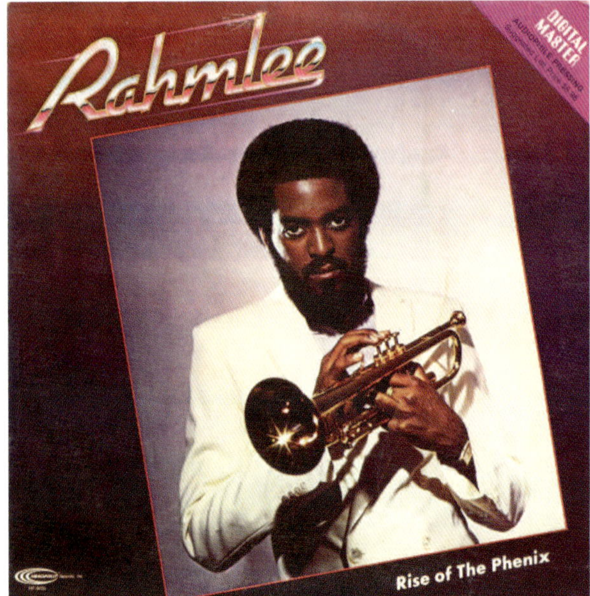

RAHMLEE Rise Of The Phenix **Headfirst** 1981 **Art Direction by** Syl Brown **Design by** Craig Jones **Photography by** Diana Lyn

AMINA CLAUDINE MYERS TRIO The Circle Of Time **Black Saint** 1984
Cover Artwork by Pick Up Studios **Photography by** Alice Su

NINA SIMONE Nina Simone With Strings **Colpix Records** 1966

ANDREW CYRILLE, JEANNE LEE & JIMMY LYONS Nuba
Black Saint 1979 **Cover Artwork & Photography by** Giuseppe Pino
Design by 'Gigi' Barbieri

BIG BLACK Ethnic Fusion **1750 Arch Records** 1982
Design by Eva Soltes **Photography by** Kris Buckner & Richard Blair
Typography by Harrington-Young Typography

GRACHAN MONCUR III & THE JAZZ COMPOSERS ORCHESTRA
Echoes Of Prayer **JCOA Records** 1975 **Layout by** Paul McDonough
Photography by Myles Walker & Alex Henderson

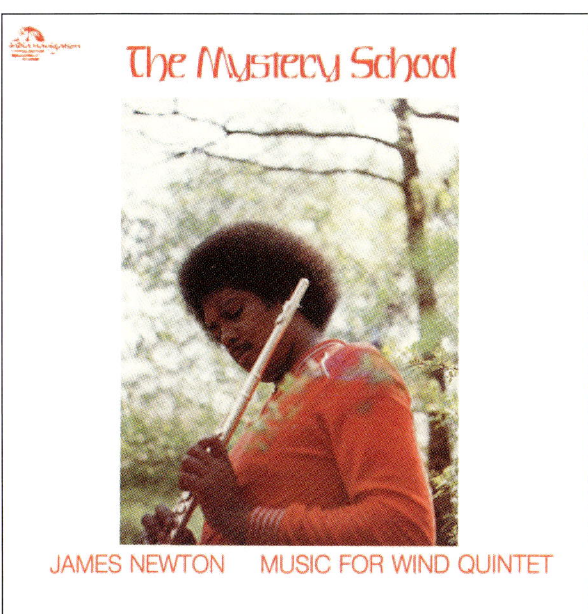

JAMES NEWTON MUSIC FOR WIND QUINTET The Mystery School **India Navigation** 1980 **Cover Artwork by** Elsie Fredricks

THE MONTGOMERY EXPRESS The Montgomery Movement **Folkways Records** 1974 **Cover Artwork by** Ronald Clyne

SOLAR PLEXUS Solar Plexus **Evidence Music International** 1975 **Design by** Pam Lingle **Calligraphy by** Judith Mieger

TERRI LYNE CARRINGTON TLC & Friends **CEI Records** 1981 **Photography by** Bill Halil

KAMAL ABDUL ALIM Dance Stash **Records** 1988 **Cover Artwork by** J.F. Ferrandez **Illustration by** Cuadrado **Photography by** Anthony Barboza

TYRONE WASHINGTON Roots **Perception Records** 1973

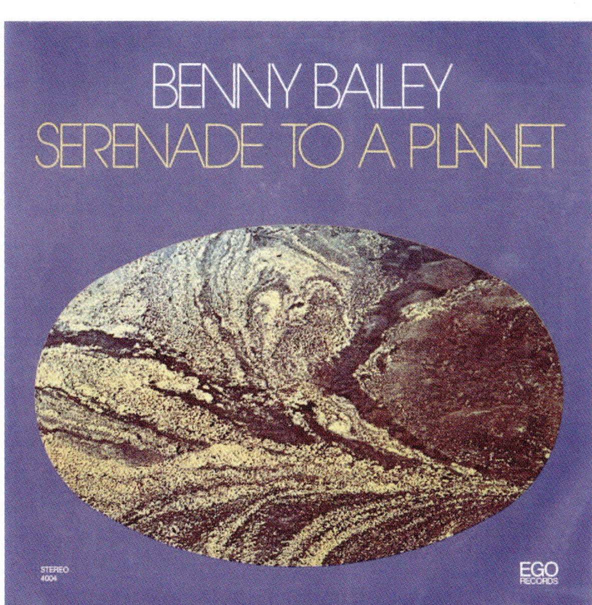

BENNY BAILEY Serenade To A Planet **EGO Records**
Cover Artwork by Josef Werkmeister **Layout by** Gabriele Fiebelkorn

CHICO FREEMAN Spirit Sensitive **India Navigation** 1979
Cover Artwork & Photography by Peter Shepherd
Layout by Beth Cummins

NEW DALTA AHKRI Song Of Humanity = Kanto Pri Homaro
Kabell Records 1977

WALTER ZUBER ARMSTRONG Alpha & Omega **World Artists Records** 1973
Cover Artwork by Sheila Miller **Photography by** Jim Breukelman

SYMPOSIUM: THE CHILDREN

EDITH HILL

SELAH

the peppered snowfall

The snow doesn't give a soft white damn Whom it touches.
— e. e. cummings

EDITH HILL SELAH Symposium: Save The Children Peppered **Snowfall Records** 1971
Photography by Mort Loveman

STEREO SES-19745

Live in Tokyo

CHARLES TOLLIVER MUSIC INC

◎ニューヨークの若獅子！ チャールズ・トリヴァー・ミュージック・INC.

11/29(木) 12/7(金) P.M. 7:00
郵便貯金ホール ● A=2,000 B=1,500

主催● FM東京 あいミュージック
後援● スイングジャーナル トリオレコード
協賛● パン・アメリカン航空
前売券は都内各プレイガイド、有名ジャズ喫茶、あいミュージックにて絶賛発売中！ お問い合せ●あいミュージック409－4727

Photo by Cairati

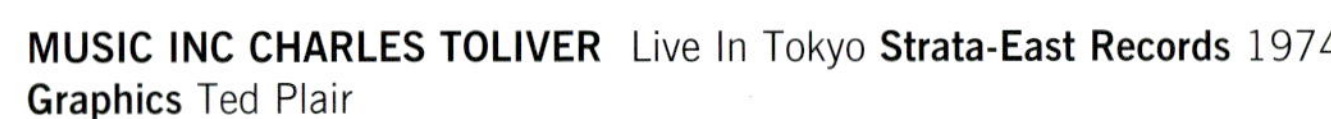

MUSIC INC CHARLES TOLIVER Live In Tokyo **Strata-East Records** 1974
Graphics Ted Plair

SAM RIVERS Crystals **Impulse! ABC Impulse! Records** 1974

LOTUS A Way of Life **Reynolds Records** 1975

STREETDANCER Future Future Records 1974
Cover Artwork Rory Bonnet

AL-FATIHAHSalaam Record Corp 1969
Photography by Gerald's Photo Art Studio

REVOLUTIONARY ENSEMBLE

Jerome Cooper/percussion

Sirone/bass

Leroy Jenkins/violin

REVOLUTIONARY ENSEMBLE ESP Records 1972
Cover Artwork by Matthew Klein **Photography by** Matthew Klein

BETTER BOYS FOUNDATION FAMILY CENTRE PRESENTS BLACK FAIRY **Better Boys Foundation Family Centre** 1975

RASHIED ALI QUARTET New Directions In Modern Music **Survival Records** 1973
Cover Artwork by Rashied Ali **Photography by** Ray Gibson

FREEDOM RECORDS

Producer Alan Bates formed Black Lion Records in London in 1968. Initially released through Polydor, the label became independent in 1971. Bates recorded visiting American artists including Dexter Gordon, Illinois Jacquet, Earl Hines, Ben Webster and others as well as releasing music from Charles Tolliver and Sun Ra ('Pictures of Infinity' (1971)).

In 1971 Bates launched a second label, Freedom, as a subsidiary of Black Lion, again recording Americans in Europe, the US and England, but focussed solely on free and forward-thinking jazz artists. In the first four years of the label, Bates created an impressive catalogue of releases that included new music by Cecil Taylor, Albert Ayler, Ornette Coleman, Anthony Braxton, Noah Howard, Stanley Cowell, The Art Ensemble of Chicago and others.

In 1975, Freedom was bought by New York-based major label Arista Records. After record executive Clive Davis was fired from CBS, he was hired by Columbia Pictures to head-up a new record division, Arista Records, which launched in 1974 with a ten million dollar investment from the parent company. While Arista was focussed on pop and rock acts, Arista/Freedom was focussed on free jazz.

Building on the original Freedom catalogue, Arista continued the label's early legacy by releasing a string of free jazz albums comprised of new recordings, re-releases of the earlier catalogue titles, and a number of albums recorded at the Montreux Jazz Festival in 1974. Artists included Andrew Hill, Oliver lake, Cecil Taylor, Noah Howard, Julius Hemphill, Frank Lowe, The Human Arts Ensemble and more.

Perhaps it's a little ironic that some of the most 'outside' recordings of free jazz were released by Arista Records, a powerful major commercial record company. Or perhaps not; in the fifteen years since the creation of free jazz, artists had radically transformed their relationship with the music industry. ESP-Disk's slogan 'The artists alone decide what you hear …', was a phrase that could now be applied to even the most established record companies.

By the end of the 1970s, parent company Columbia Pictures was in trouble financially, and, in order stave off bankruptcy, Arista was sold to German-based Ariola Records in 1979 at which point Freedom became a catalogue label.

JULIUS HEMPHILL 'Coon Bid'Ness **Freedom Records** 1975
Cover Artwork by Bill Hoffman **Photography by** Ron Warwell

CECIL TAYLOR What's New **Freedom Records** 1974
Cover Artwork by Hamish Grimes **Photography by** Jan Persson

FRANK LOWE Fresh **Freedom Records** 1975 **Cover Artwork** Frank Roth **Design by** Bob Heimall **Photography by** Raymond Ross

ARCHIE SHEPP There's A Trumpet In My Soul **Freedom Records** 1975 **Artwork by** Nelson Stevens **Design by** Nancy Greenberg **Photography by** Raymond Ross

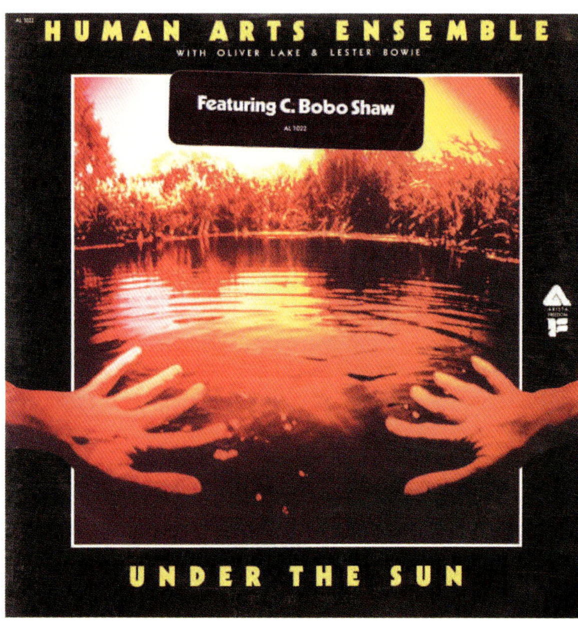

HUMAN ARTS ENSEMBLE Under The Sun **Freedom Records** 1975
Cover Artwork Mary Walsh **Design** Bob Heimall
Photography by Raymond Ross

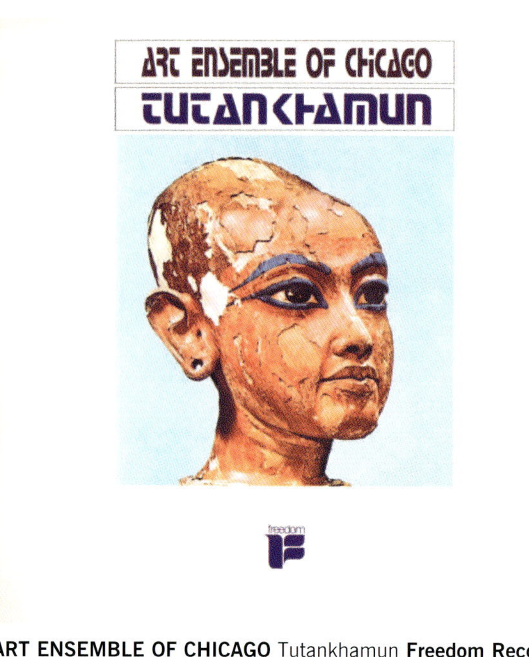

ART ENSEMBLE OF CHICAGO Tutankhamun **Freedom Records** 1974
Cover Artwor byk Hamish Grimes

STANLEY COWELL

BRILLIANT CIRCLES

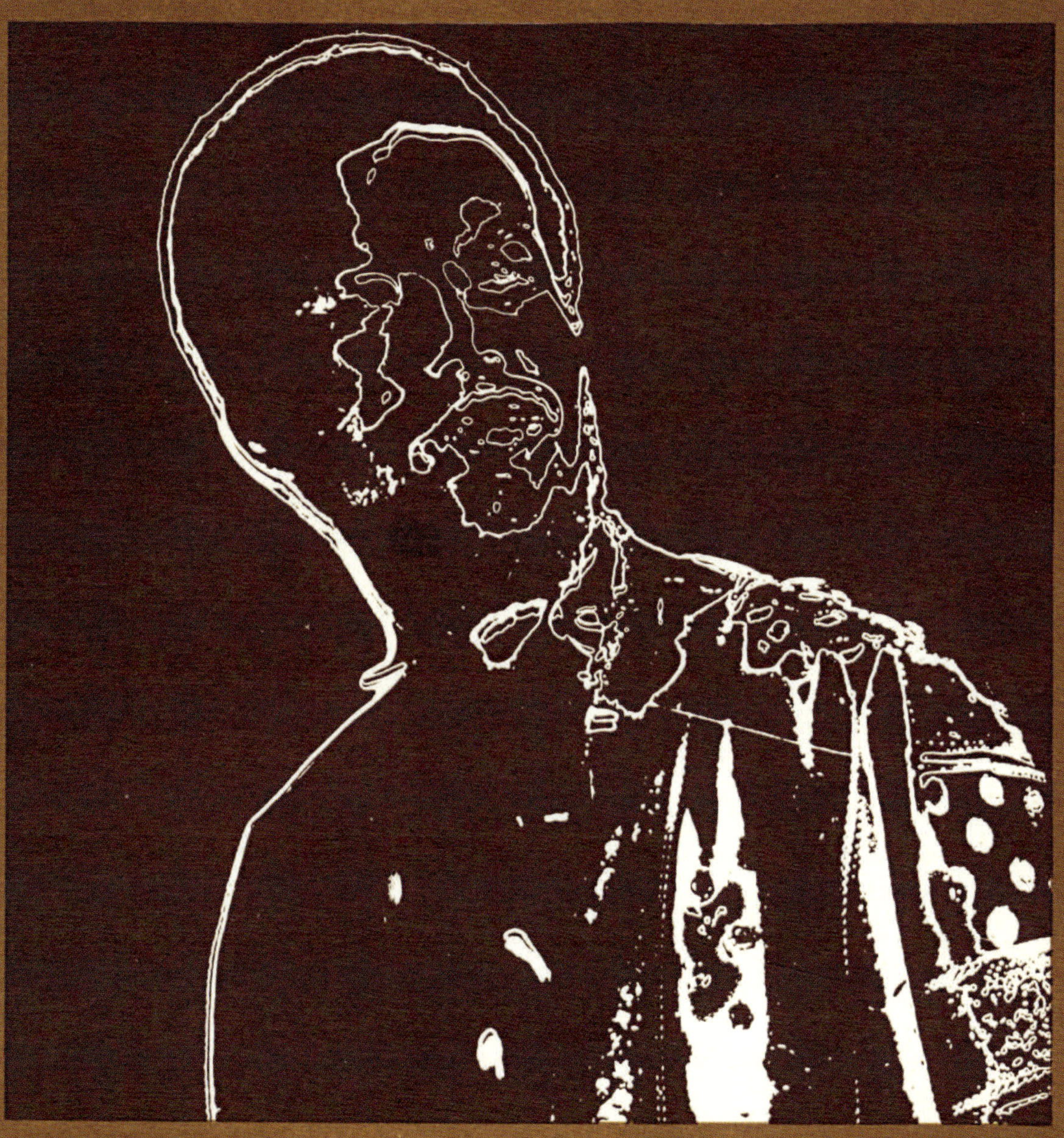

STANLEY COWELL Brilliant Circles **Freedom Records** 1972
Cover Artwork by Hamish Grimes **Photography by** Charles Stewart **Graphics by** Phillip Gotlop

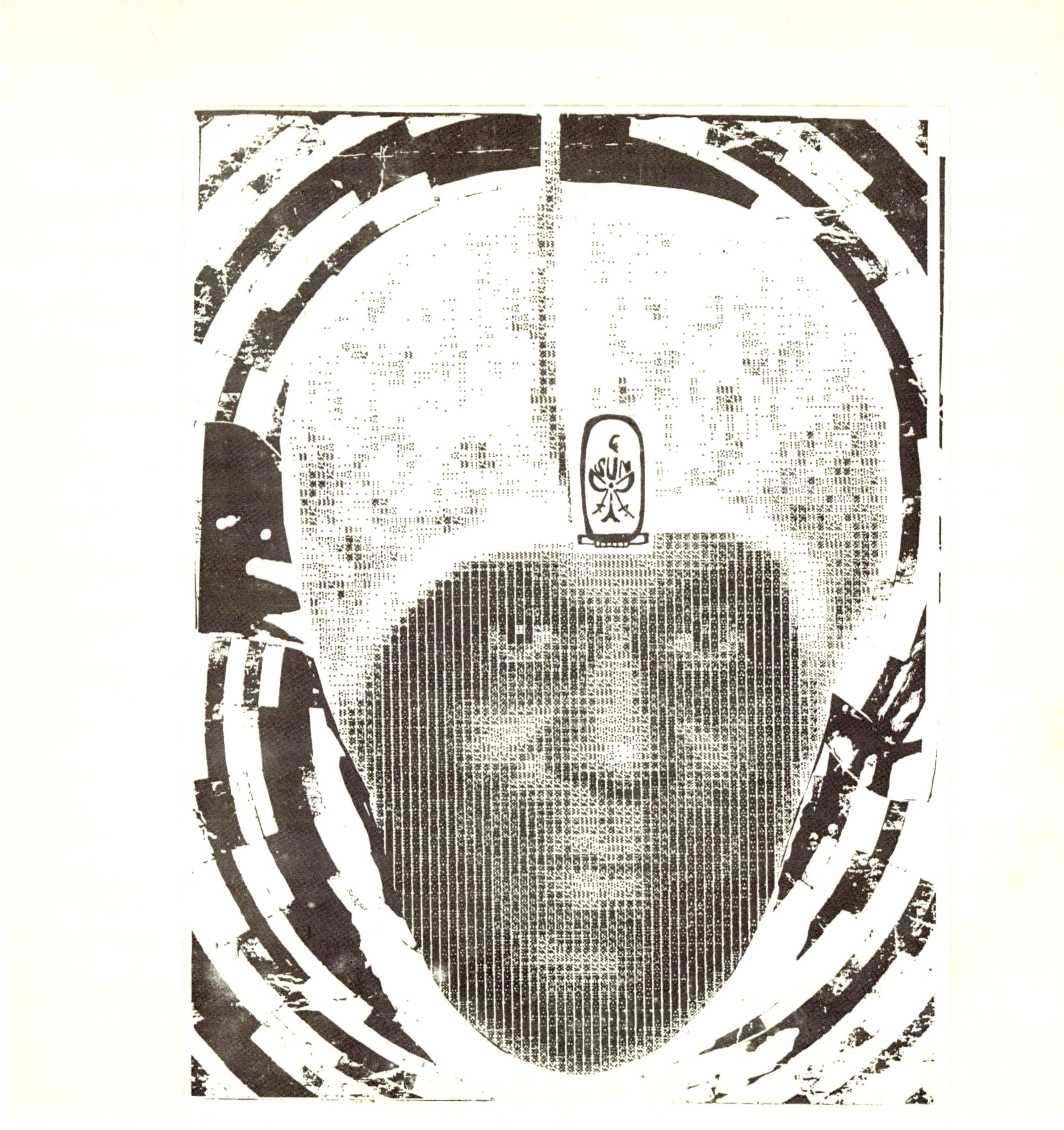

SUN RA AND HIS OUTER SPACE ARKESTRA On Jupiter **El Saturn Records** 1979
Photocopied hand made sleeve

IKE ISAACS At Freddie Jett's Pied Piper **Black Saint Soul Note RGB Records** 1969
Photography by Ray Avery

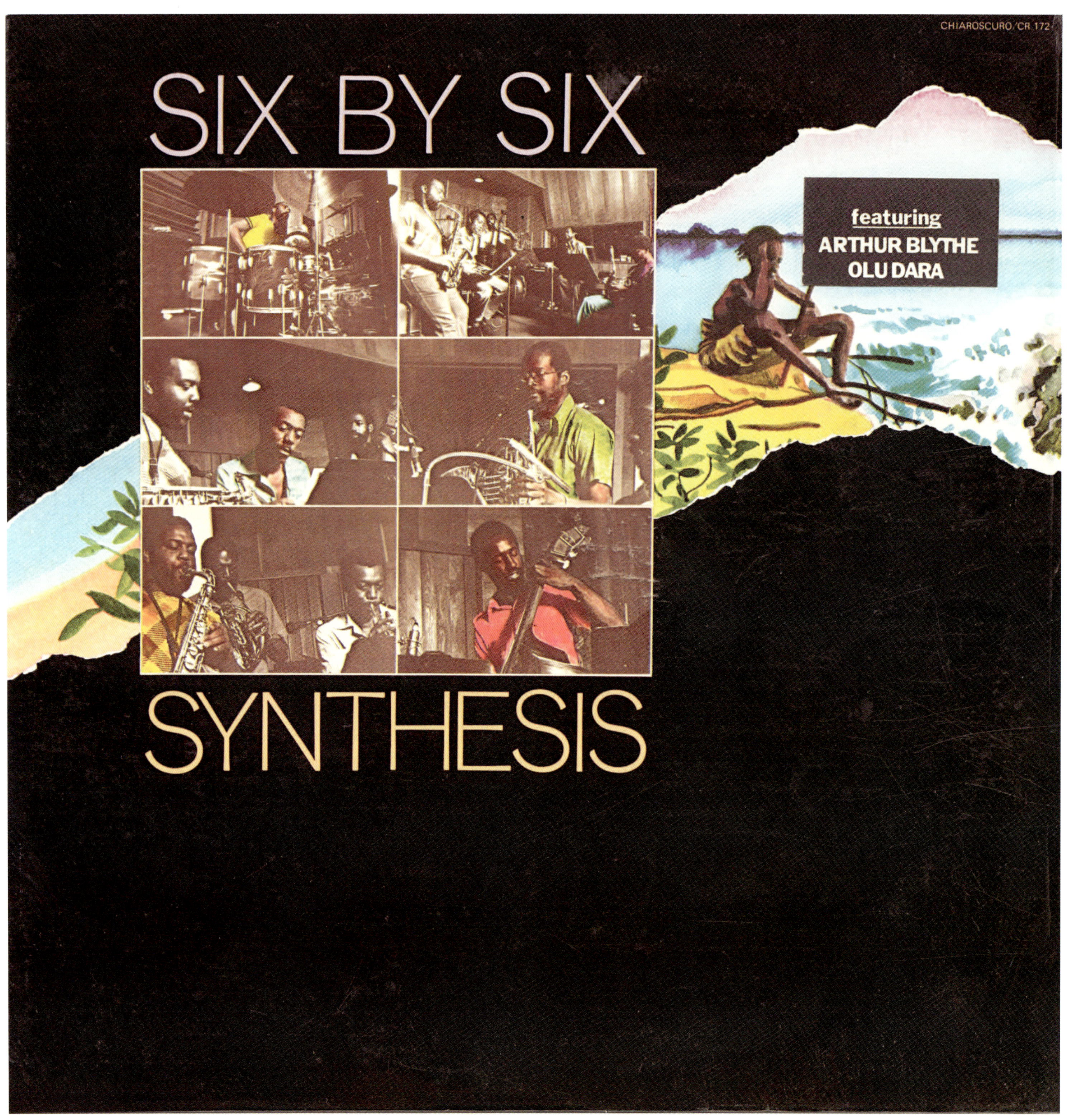

SYNTHESIS Six By Six **Chiaroscuro Records** 1977
Cover Artwork by Ron Warwell **Photography by** Clarence Eastmond

DOUG & JEAN CARN
HIGHER GROUND

DOUG & JEAN CARN Higher Ground **Ovation Records** 1976
Cover Artwork by Rob Dorobiala **Design by** Jerry Napier

SUN-RA AND HIS ASTRO INFINITY ARKESTRA My Brother The Wind **Saturn Research Records** 1970
(Hand-coloured)

SUN RA AND HIS ARKESTRA Sound Mirror **El Saturn Records** 1978

STEEPLECHASE RECORDS

SteepleChase Records was founded in Copenhagen, Denmark, in 1972 by Nils Winther. A number of American jazz musicians lived in Copenhagen including Stan Getz (whose wife was Swedish) from 1958-61, Dextor Gordon (1962-76), Ben Webster (1964-73) and Kenny Drew who moved there in 1964. The Jazzhus Montmartre became a regular venue for these and other visiting American artists.

Winther, at the time an avid jazz fan still at university, was given a room upstairs from the club and allowed to record a number of albums live at the venue. These became the first releases on SteepleChase, starting with Jackie McLean's 'Live at Montmartre'. He made his first trip to New York in 1974, recording Jackie McLean, Billy Gault and tracking down Andrew Hill. Winther built up an impressive catalogue with albums by Kenny Drew, Paul Bley, Gary Bartz, Anthony Braxton, Ken Mcintyre, Walt Dickerson, Clifford Jordan, Horace Parlan and others, taking advantage of the fact that many of these American jazz artists were no longer under contract to USA labels.

Winther also began working with younger local musicians. Many SteepleChase releases were licensed to a New York-based label, Inner City Records, giving the European label American distribution. In 1987, Steeplechase began to move towards CD production, phasing out vinyl. Unlike many other labels at the time, this did not spell the end – far from it. Their regular output of around 20 releases a year has remained unbroken for over 50 years totalling more than 1,000 to the present day, and they are pressing vinyl once more.

ONAJE ALLAN GUMBS Onaje **SteepleChase Records** 1977
Design by Per Grunnet

BILLY GAULT When Destiny Calls **SteepleChase Records** 1975
Cover Artwork by Lissa Winther

RENÉ McLEAN SEXTET Watch Out **SteepleChase** 1975
Design by Lissa Winther

HORO RECORDS

Horo Records was founded by Aldo Sinesio in Rome, Italy in 1972. Sicilian-born Sinesio had been a film director in the 1960s (such as 'Tutto il Bello dell'Uomo', made in 1963) before becoming a record producer. Horo Records ran for seven years, releasing a catalogue of high-quality releases from Sun Ra, Lester Bowie, Steve Lacy, Sam Rivers, Roy Haynes, Gil Evans, Max Roach, Archie Shepp and many others who travelled to Italy during this period.

The first release on the label was by Irio de Paula, a Brazilian composer and guitarist who had come to Italy in the group of samba singer Elsa Soares. Sinesio put him together with Mandrake Som, another Brazilian percussionist living in Rome (and Pelé's cousin!) and two Italians, Enrico Pieranunzi on piano and Alessio Urso on double bass. This became the debut release on Horo, and the first in their 'Jazz A Confronto' series. The second release featured Kenny Clarke, who was living in Paris at the time.

Horo's 'Jazz A Confronto' series featured many of the finest Italian jazz players - Gianni Basso, Giorgio Gaslini, Renato Sellani, Giorgio Barigozzi, Oscar Valdambrini, Mario Schiano, Enrico Rava, Massimo Urbani, Giancarlo Schiaffini, Enrico Pieranunzi – often together with American artists such as Frank Rosolino and Kenny Clarke. Most of the catalogue has remained out of print ever since their initial releases more than 40 years ago.

KENNY CLARKE Jazz A Confronto 20 **Horo Records** 1975
Design by Pierro Gratton **Photography by** Aldo Sinesio

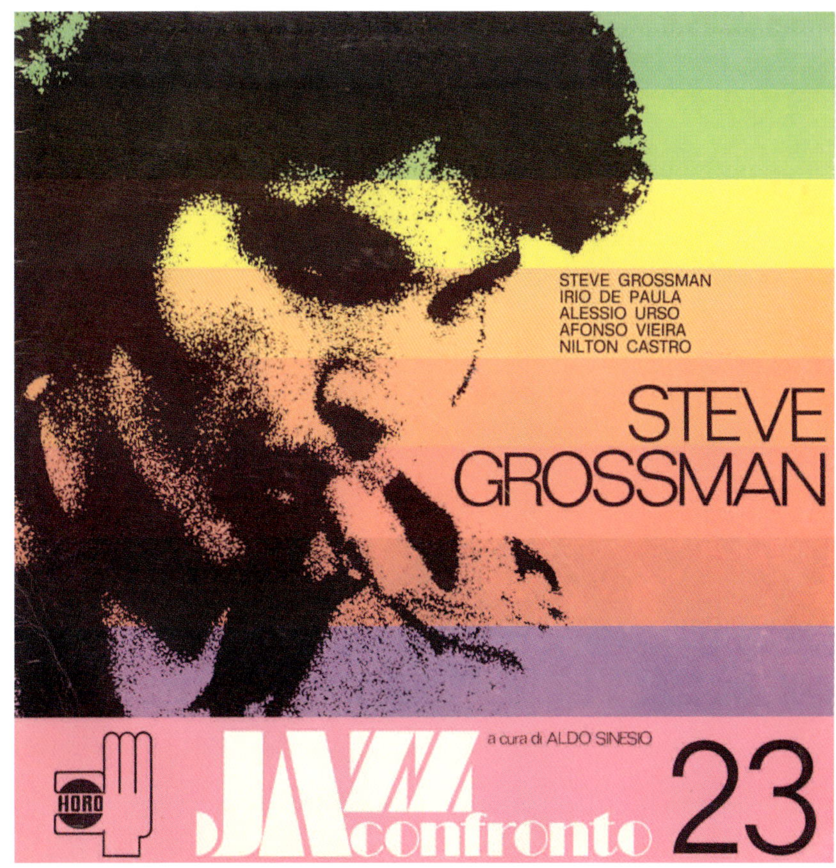

STEVE GROSSMAN Jazz A Confronto 23 **Horo Records** 1975
Design by Pierro Gratton **Photography by** Isio Saba

ARCHIE SHEPP

& THE NEW YORK CONTEMPORARY FIVE

WHERE POPPIES BLOOM

LIKE A BLESSED BABY LAMB

CONSEQUENCES

COMPOSED AND ARRANGED BY ARCHIE SHEPP

TENOR SAXOPHONE: ARCHIE SHEPP
ALTO SAXOPHONE: JOHN TCHICAI
TRUMPET: DON CHERRY
BASS: RONNIE BOYKINS
DRUMS: SONNY MURRAY

GUEST ARTIST—
TED CURSON: TRUMPET

BILL DIXON 7-TETTE

THE 12TH DECEMBER

WINTER SONG 1964

COMPOSED AND ARRANGED BY BILL DIXON

TRUMPET: BILL DIXON
TENOR SAXOPHONE: GEORGE BARROW
ALTO SAXOPHONE AND OBOE: KEN McINTYRE
TUBA AND BARITONE: HOWARD JOHNSON
BASSES: DAVE IZENSON, HAL DODSON
DRUMS: HOWARD McRAE

ARCHIE SHEPP & THE NEW YORK CONTEMPORARY FIVE Savoy Records 1964
Photography by Olé

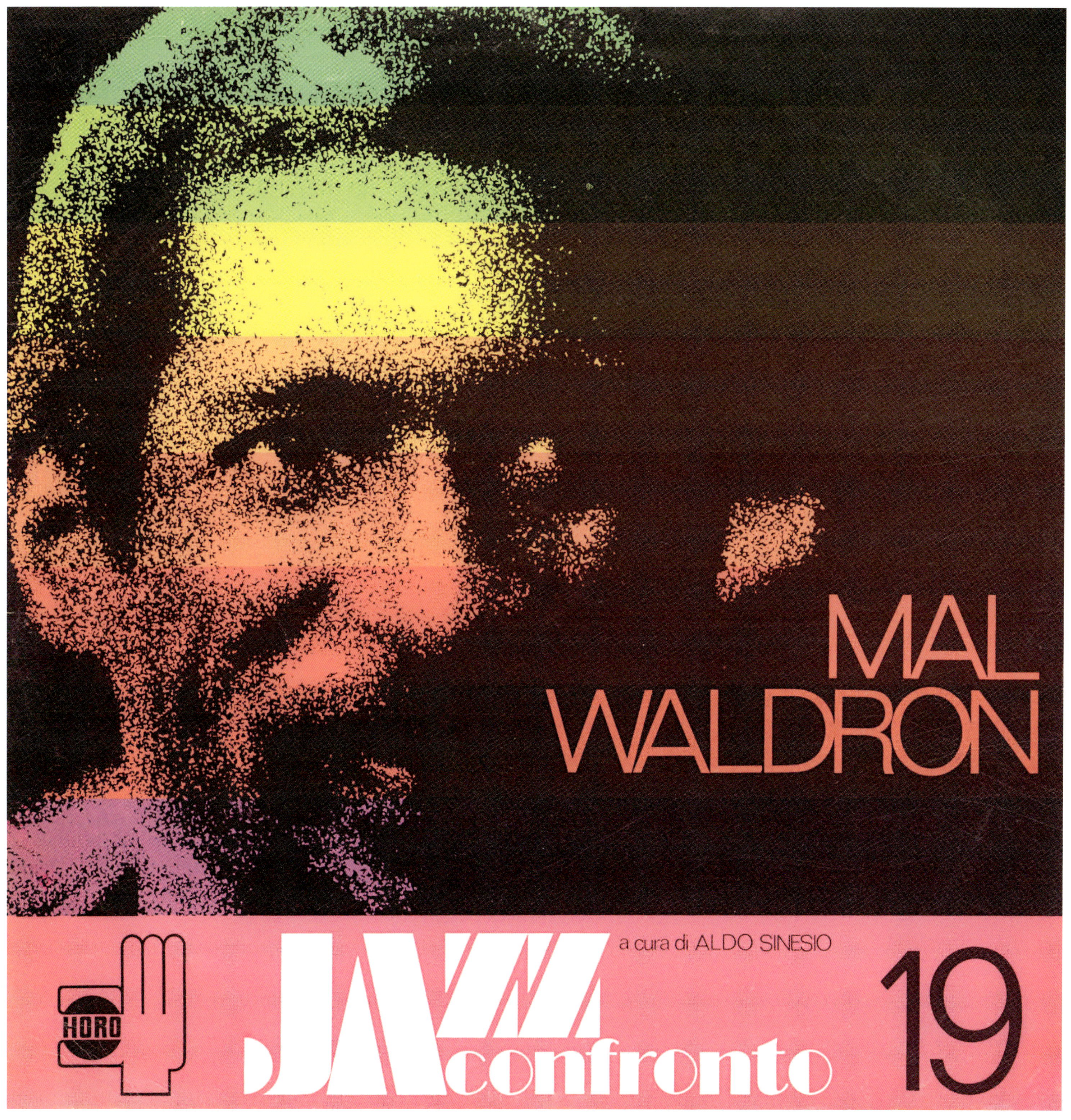

MAL WALDRON Jazz A Confronto 19 **Horo Records** 1975
Cover Artwork by Piero Gratton **Photograph by** Pepito Pegnatelli

THE SEARCH

CHICO FREEMAN

CHICO FREEMAN The Search **India Navigation Records** 1983
Cover Artwork by Tan Ohe **Photography by** Beth Cummins

JUNCTION

ANDREW CYRILLE & Māōnō

with
David Ware
Ted Daniel
Lisle Atkinson

ANDREW CYRILLE & MĀŌNO Junction **IPS Records** 1976
Cover Artwork by Dawoud Bey **Photography by** Dawoud Bey

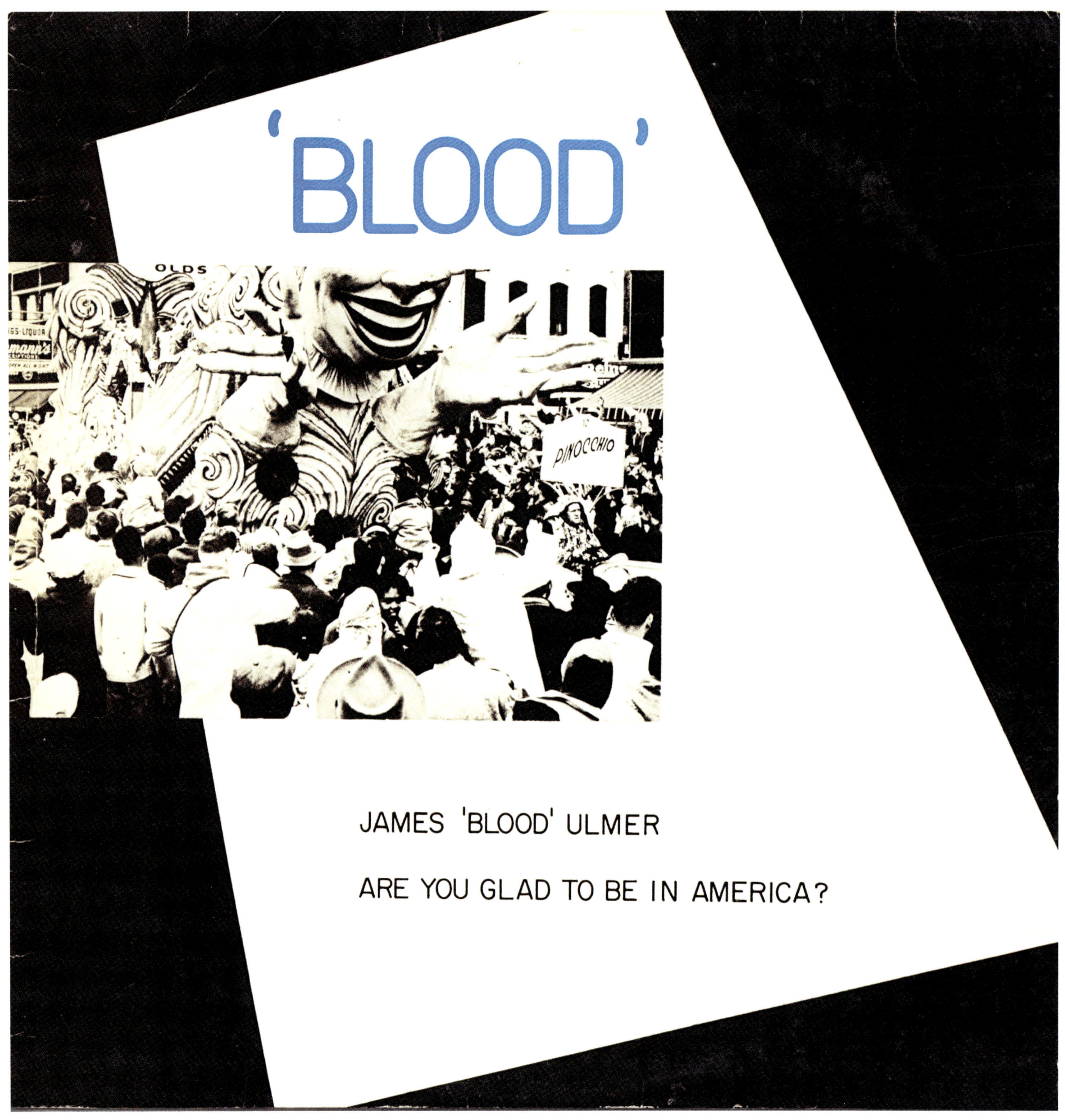

BLOOD' JAMES 'BLOOD' ULMMER Are You Glad To Be In America? **Rough Trade Records** 1980

ARCHIE SHEPP/BILL DIXON Consequences **BYG Records**
Cover Artwork by Pierre Bompar **Photography by** Joe Alter

DOUGLAS HARPER'S JAZZ FRIENDS April Jam **Open Reel Records** 1980 **Cover Artwork by** Bo Odén **Photography by** Matts Lindblad

ERROL PARKER My Own Bag **Sahara Records** 1972 **Photography by** Claude Fitte

SHANNON JACKSON & THE DECODING SOCIETY Nasty **Moers Music** **Photography by** Deborah Feingold

RON CARTER Very Well **Polydor Records** 1987 **Cover Artwork by** Takasi Ito **Photography by** Masayoshi Sukita

NATHEN PAGE Page-ing Nathan **Hugo's Music** 1982 **Cover Artwor byk** Rick Kann **Photography by** Bob Egerton

DANA KAPROFF 1976 **Cover Artwork by** Laurence Starkman

KHAN JAMAL QUARTET Dark Warrior **SteepleChase Records** 1984 **Cover Artwork by** Per Grunt **Photography by** Nils Winther

SONNY AND LINDA SHARROCK Paradise **Atco Records** 1975 **Cover Artwork by** Paula Scher **Photograph by** Jim Houghton and Earl Steinbicker

GREG ADAMS Gemini **Jazz Beat Records** 1984 **Photograph by** Yvonne M Adams

CAVRIL PAYNE Cavril Sings **Ruval Records** 1971
Photography by Maurice Seymour

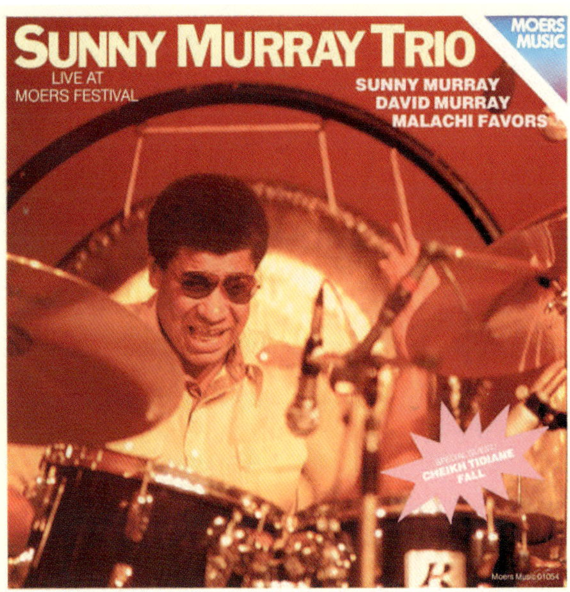

SUNNY MURRAY TRIO Live at Moers Festival **Moers Music** 1979
Cover Artwork by Jürgen Pankarz **Photography by** Ralph Quinke

PRINCE LAWSHA Firebirds Live At Monterey Jazz Festival Vol III **Birdseye Records** 1976 **Cover Artwork by** Padreigin McGillicuddy & Mary Lawsha

POTTER AND TILLMAN New York to LA :Coasting **Poet Records** 1980
Cover Artwork by Philip Greenberg **Photography by** David Greenberg

BUSTER WILLIAMS Pinnacle **Muse Records** 1975
Cover Artwork by Doug Dunn **Photography by** Price Givens

CLIFFORD JORDAN AND THE MAGIC TRIANGLE The Highest Mountain
Inner City/SteepleChase Records 1976 **Cover Artwork by** Lissa Winther

DAVID MURRAY OCTET Ming **Black Saint** 1980
Cover Artwork by "Gigi" Barbieri **Photography by** Trevor Brown

FRANCISCO MORA Mora! **AACE Records** 1985
Cover Artwork & Photography by Mary Luevanos

NORMAN WILLIAMS The One Mind Experience **The Bishop Theresa Records** 1977 **Cover Artwork by** Frank Vega **Photography by** Dennis Sharp

SUNRISE LTD Until My Love Returns **Pizzazz Records** 1980

CHOSEN FEW Moments of the Past **Phonograph Records** 1982

THE REVOLUTIONARY ENSEMBLE Manhattan Cycles **India Navigation** 1973
Design by TAMADAH **Photography by** Bob Cummins

SUN RA AND HIS ARKESTRA Dance Of Innocent Passion **El Saturn** 1981

ECM RECORDS

The independent record label ECM – Edition of Contemporary Music – was founded by producer Manfred Eicher in Munich, Germany in 1969. To date ECM has released over 1700 albums.

Eicher had studied double bass in Berlin and worked as a production assistant at the highly-regarded classical label, Deutsche Grammophon. When he launched ECM he bought these exacting standards to recording improvised music. The first releases on the label were Mal Waldron's 'Free at Last' and Marion Brown's 'Afternoon of a Georgia Faun'. ECM established its reputation with many excellent records by pioneering artists from around the world: From the USA Keith Jarrett, Chick Corea, Paul Bley, Gary Burton, Pat Metheny, Jack DeJohnette and the Art Ensemble of Chicago; from Brazil Nana Vasconceles, Egberto Gismonti; from Norway saxophonist Jan Garbarek and many others.

By the end of the 1970s modern composers such as Meredith Monk and Steve Reich also regularly recorded on ECM. The label has continued to look forward, creating an identity that crosses many areas of music that somehow always remains unmistakeable and yet undefined. Part of this is due to the iconic record sleeve artwork (minimal, surreal, painterly) from designers Barbara Wojirsch (originally with her husband Burkhart Wojirsch until his death in the mid-70s), and later Dieter Rehm and Sascha Kleis always working in collaboration with founder and producer Manfred Eicher.

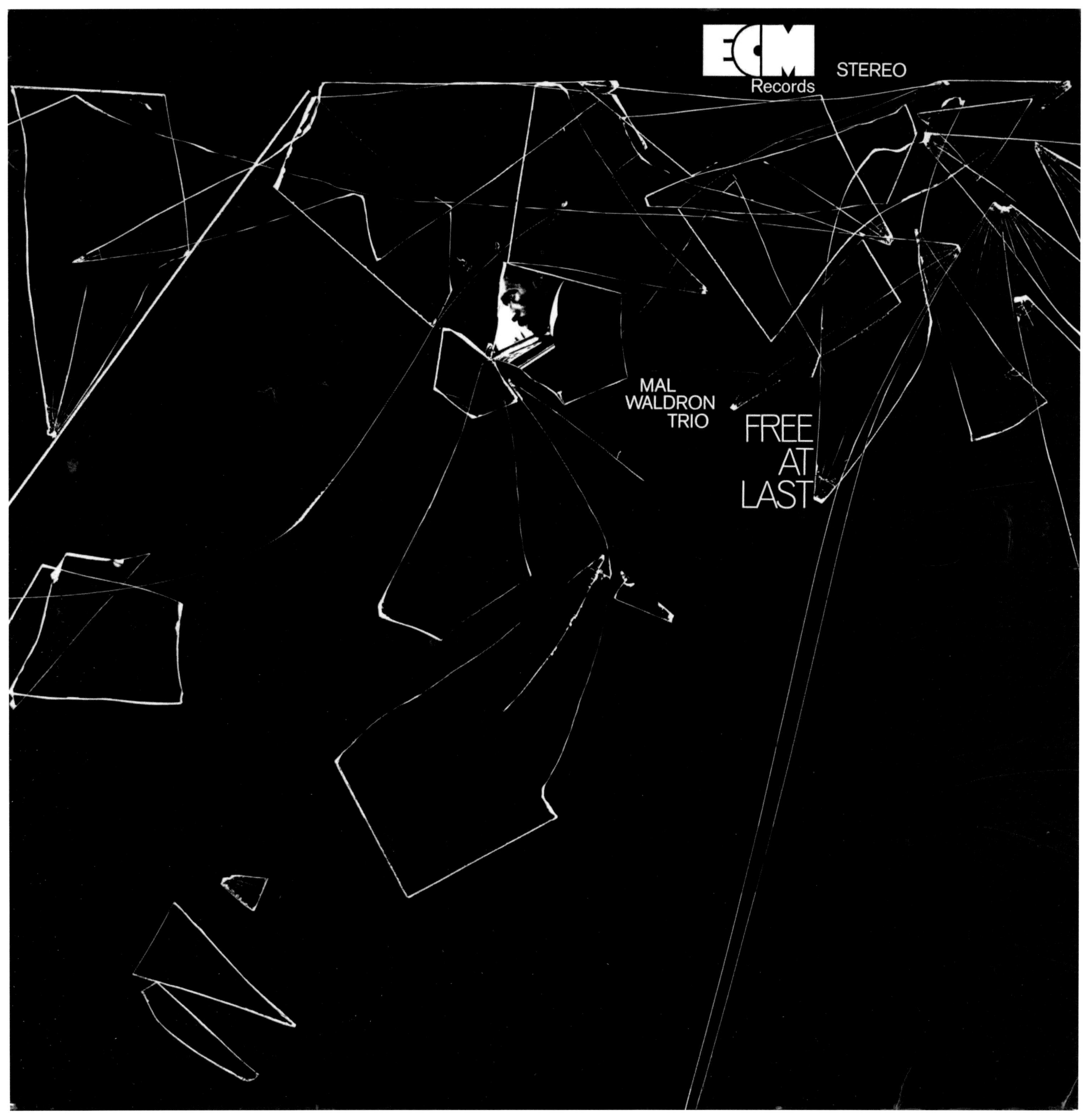

MAL WALDRON TRIO Free At Last **ECM Records** 1970
Cover Artwork by Rufus Vedder

MARION BROWN Afternoon Of A Georgia Faun **ECM Records** 1970
Cover Artwork by Dieter Henkel

DOUG HAMMOND AND MO' FOLKS We People **Idlib Records** 1989
Cover Artwork by Allen Colding

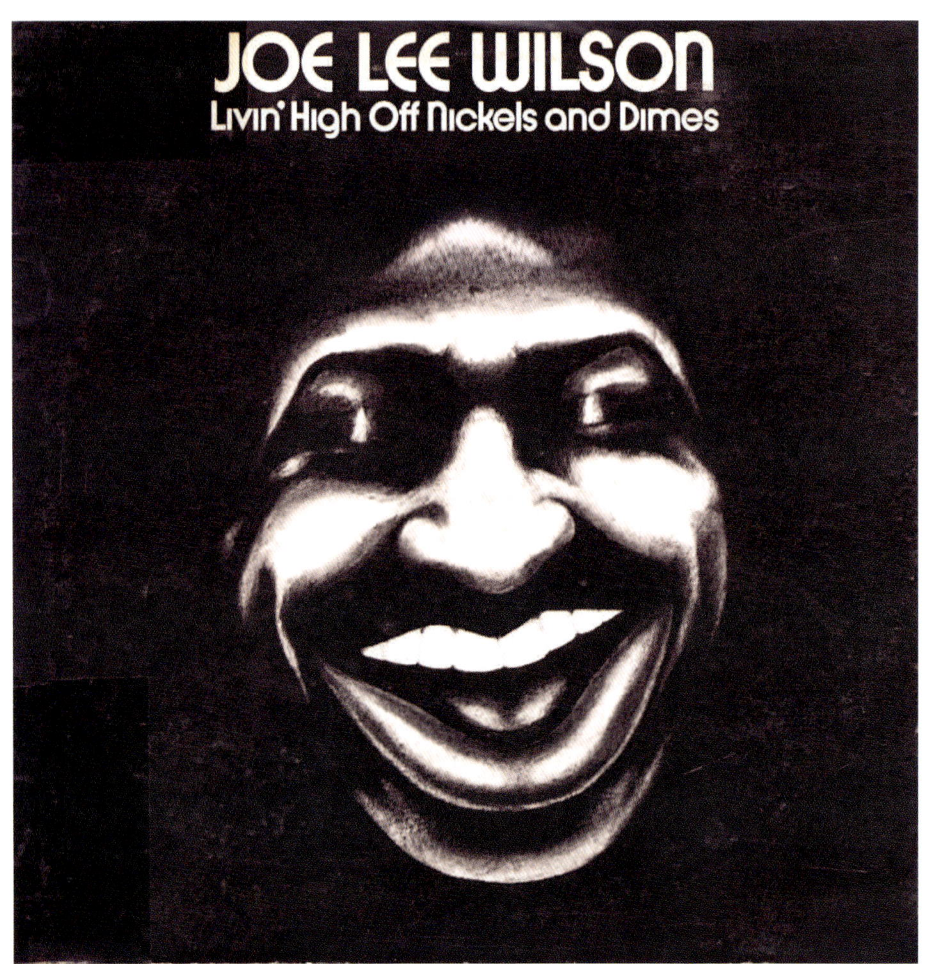

JOE LEE WILSON Livin' High Off Nickels And Dimes **Oblivion Records** 1974
Cover Artwork by Susan Rivoir **Graphics by** Oblivionettes **Photography by** Bridget Deale

GARY BIAS East 101 **Nimbus West Records** 1981
Cover Artwork by Avery Clayton **Photography by** John Frazier

JOE CHAMBERS New World **Finite Finite Records** 1976 **Cover Artwork by** Elise Irby **Photography by** Joan Lichtig

ART ENSEMBLE OF CHICAGO Phase One **Prestige Records** 1973 **Cover Artwork by** Tony Lane **Design by** Jamie Putnam **Photography by** Gilbert Moreau

ORNETTE COLEMAN Crisis **Impulse! Records** 1972 **Cover Artwork by** George Whiteman **Photography by** George Whiteman

ROACH OM Universal Expressions **United Sound Records** 1972

ANTHONY DAVIS / JAMES NEWTON QUARTET Hidden Voices **India Navigation Records** 1979

EUROPEAN PRIVATE AND INDEPENDENT PRESS

When The Art Ensemble of Chicago and the other new wave of African-American jazz artists arrived in Europe, many at the end of the 1960s, they found an excited public waiting to hear them perform live. They also instigated a nascent independent record industry eager to work with them and record their music.

Many European musicians came under their influence – musically, but also philosophically, absorbing some of the inter-connected ideas of the Black Power Movement carried by these African-American musicians: self-determination, the creation of independent political and cultural institutions, economic empowerment, and a sense of collective identity.

This led to a number of European artists releasing their own music privately. Similar to the situation in the USA, without the weight of the music industry, many of these records remain under the radar, but possess an integrity in sound that few commercial releases could match.

B. P. CONVENTION, ZAGREBAČKI SOLISTI Misterij Bluesa (Mistery Of Blues) **Jugoton Records** 1976
Cover Artwork by Edo Murtić **Photography by** Ivo Ivezeć

BOBO STENSON ARILD ANDERSEN JON CHRISTENSEN Underwear **ECM Records** 1971 **Cover Artwork by** B & B Wojirsch **Photography by** H. Cananis

ATARPOP 73 & LE COLLECTIF LE TEMPS DES CERISES Attention **L'Armée Temps des Cerises Records** 1975 **Cover Art by** Atarpop 73

LLOYD MILLER Near And Far East **East West Records** 1966

DOGLIOTTI Canoombe For Export **Sunday Records** 1970 **Cover Artwork by** Julio Testoni **Photography by** Julio Testoni

SERGIO FANNI QUINTET Hard Suite **Carosello Records** 1975

GUSTANO BERGALLI QUINTET Dragon Records 1986

FRANÇOIS TUSQUES & INTERCOMMUNAL FREE DANCE MUSIC ORCHESTRA Après La Marée Noire - Vers Une Musique Bretonne Nouvelle **Le Chant du Monde Records** 1979 **Cover Artwork by** Stéfan Thanneur & Anne Marie Dufour **Photography by** Michel Popovic

DIETER REITH CHARLY ANTOLINI PETER WITTLE A Happy Afternoon **SABA Records** 1966

CASCADA Cascade **Chambacú** 1980 **Cover Artwork by** Philip M Awuy

JOHN THOMAS & LIFEFORCE 3000 Worlds **Nabel Records** 1981
Cover Artwork by Rainer Wiedensohler **Photography by** Rainer Gillesen

FRANCO AMBROSETTI Horo Records 1974 **Cover Artwork by** Giorgio Spadanuda **Photography by** Ennio Antonangeli

EERO KOIVISTOINEN KVINTETTI & SEKSTETTI Odysseus
4Kustannusosakeyhtiö Otava Records 1969 **Cover Artwork by** Harri Manner

ALLEGRO JAZZ BAND The Golden Mean **Мелодия Records** 1985
Cover Artwork by Борис Дударев **Photography** А. Малахин Г. Прохоров

LENA LESCA Projection Vie **Lena Lesca Records** 1978
Cover Artwork by Eve **Photography by** Jean Michel Gautier

BRIGITTE FONTAINE Saravah Records 1972
Photography by Ned Burgess

COÏNCIDENCE Disques Tremble 1977
Cover Artwork by Bernard Fernandez **Photography by** Alain Fabre

POTEMKINE Foetus **Pôle Records** 1976
Photography by Alain Lahana

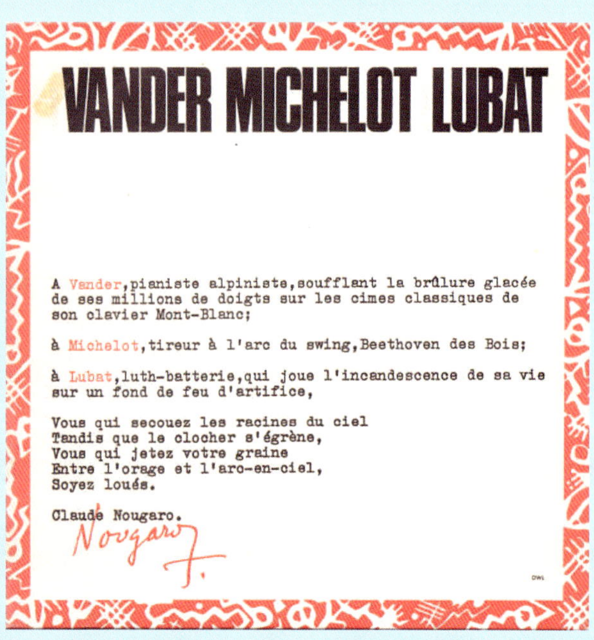

VANDER MICHELOT LUBAT Owl Records 1985
Cover Artwork by Bernard Amiard **Photography By** Gilles Ehrmann

THE THEO LOEVENDIE CONSORT Mandela **Catfish Records** 1970
Cover Artwork by Jan Fijnheer

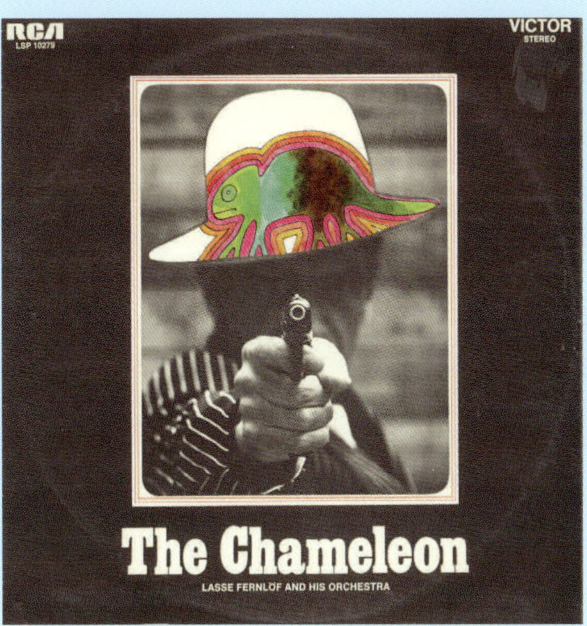

LASSE FERNLÖF AND HIS ORCHESTRA The Chameleon **RCA Victor Records** 1969

OLLI AHVENLAHTI Bandstand **Love Records** 1975
Cover Artwork by Anita Westin

PETER STRØMBERGS KVARTET Strømme **EMI Parlophone Records** 1971
Cover Artwork by Flemming Quist Møller **Photography by** Susanne Mertz

VARIOUS ARTISTS Jazz In Basel **Swiss Jazz Records** 1965
Cover Artwork by F Milani

PATRICE GELSI Ailleurs... 1983
Photography by Jean-Christophe Paris

TRIO MANUSARDI Impresii Din Vacanță **Electrecord Records** 1974
Photography by Nicolae Mihăilescu

MUSICA HELVETICA SBC Swiss Broadcasting Corporation Records 1976 **Cover Artwork by** Hans Erni **Design by** Colin Farmer

PERIGEO Azimut **RCA Italiana Records** 1972
Cover Artwork by Up & Down Studio

THE BARON VON OHLEN QUARTET FEATURING MARY ANN MOSS The Baron **Creative World** 1973 **Photography by** Noble Bretzman Studios

KOMEDA QUINTET Astigmatic Polskie **Nagrania Muza** 1967 **Cover Artwork by** Roslaw Szaybo

GINO MARINACCI Gino Marinacci **Idea Records** 1976

IVAN OSCARSSON & CONSORTES Ivan The Terrible **Dragon Records** 1976 **Photography by** Hofdhi Sammouda

GEORGE GRUNTZ Noon In Tunisia **SABA** 1967 **Photography by** German Hasenfratz and Josef Werkmeister

CAST s/t **Ciao** 1980 **Cover Artwork, Art Direction & Design by** Antonella Italiani **Photography & Cover Concept by** Walter Calloni

PIERO UMLIANI Jazz a Confronto 35 **Horo Records** 1977 **Cover Artwork by** Sandro Lodolo

FRANCY BOLAND Jazz Joint Volume 1 'Going Classic' **Vogue Schallplaten** 1971 **Cover Artwork by** Hanel Design **by** Heinz Bähr

VARIOUS ARTISTS Naissus Jazz '81 **Diskos** 1982 **Photography by** Miomir-Magdevski

ENZO RANDISI s/t **P..D.R.** 1978

RENATO SELLANI TRIO Piazza S. Eufemia **PDU** 1974

MAFFY FALAY / SEVDA s/t **Caprice Records** 1972
Cover Artwork & Layout by Gunnar Erkner

MISA BLAM Sećanja **Bograd Disk** 1980
Design & Photography by Branislav-Petković

NICOS JARITZ UNIDAD Para Los Compañeros **Kovarik's Musikothek** 1985
Cover Artwork by Ferdinand Lenartitsch

JOACHIM-KÜHN FEATURING ALPHONSE-MOUZON Hip Elegy **MPS / BASF** 1976 **Cover Artwork by** Gabriele Laurenz

PROPAGANDA Apatija Javnosti **PGP RTB** 1982

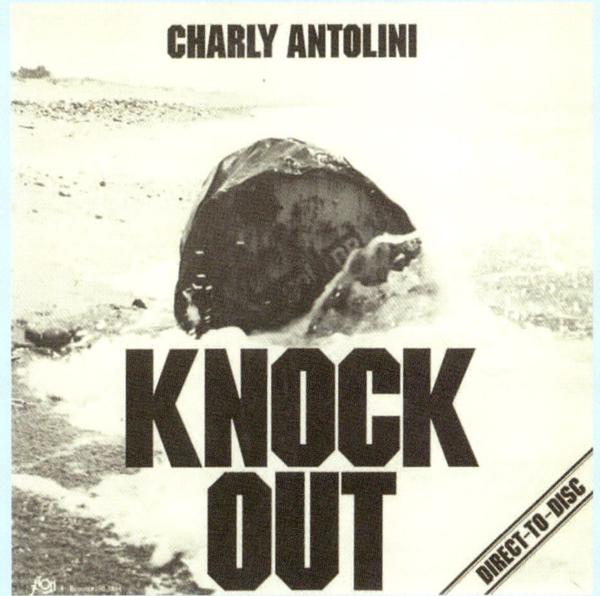

CHARLY ANTOLINI Knock Out **Jeton** 1979

TONE JANŠA JAZZ KVARTET s/t **PGP RTB** 1977
Photography by

ARDE MEN SESTETTO BASSO VALDAMBRINI
The Best Modern Jazz in Italy 1962

NATHAN DAVIS QUINTET FEATURING CARMELL JONES The Hip Walk **MPS Records** 1971 (Original SABA 1965)

PALLE MIKKELBORG & RADIOJAZZGRUPPEN The Mysterious Corona
Debut Records 1967 **Photography by** Jan Persson

SABU MARTINEZ Afro Temple **Grammofonverket** 1973
Design Lorne De Wolfe

CHARLES 'LOLO' BELLONZI QUARTET FEATURING GLENN FERRIS
Night and Day 1981

JAYSON LINDH Second Carneval **JAS Records** 1975
Cover Photography by Tim Moriarty

QUINTETTO SANTUCCI-SCOPPa Looking Around **Fly Records** 1971

GUNTER HAMPEL QUINTET Heartplants **SABA** 1965
Photography by Josef Werkmeister

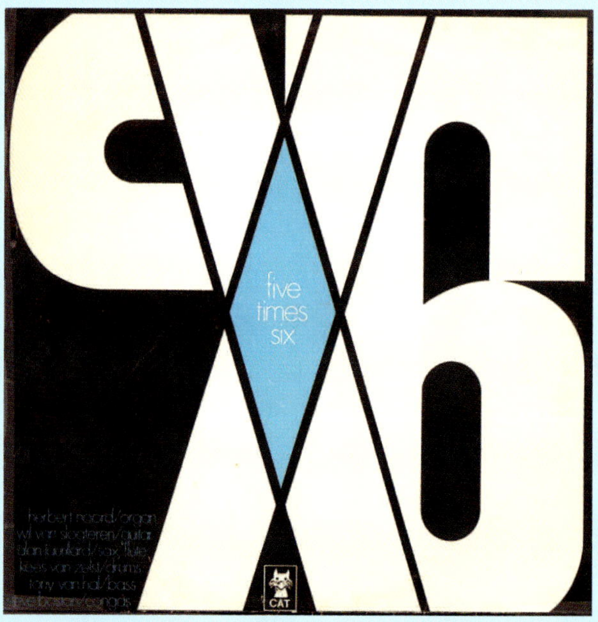

FIVE TIMES SIX Five Times Six **Cat Records** 1974
Cover Design Wil Van Slogteren

ACHIM KÜCK & FRIENDS Scurrility **Blind Man Music** 1982
Cover Artwork by Hans Clauss

TORDENSKJOLDS SOLDATER Peace **Spectator Records** 1970
Cover Artwork by Birgit Schmidt

COSSI ANATZ Jazz **Disques Vendémiaire**
Cover Artwork by Francine Gaspar Jean-Pierre Graziani

MUSICA ORBIS To The Listeners **Longevity Records** 1977

JERZY MILIAN Orkiestra Rozrywkowa PRiTV w Katowicach **Polskie Nagrania Muza** 1975

JANA KOUBKOVÁ Bossa **Supraphon/Gramofonový Klub** 1985
Design by Jiří Eliška

BASSO-VALDAMBRINI SEXTET Exciting 6 **GTA Records** 1966

MICHAEL GARRICK SEXTET Jazz Praises **Airborne Records** 1968

RENATO SELLANI Horo Records
Cover Artwork by Giorgio Spadanuda **Photography by** Ennio Antonangeli

Plunky and Oneness of Ju Ju

Introducing

Virtania Tillery

ELECTRIC
JU JU
NATION

Special Edition Double Artist LP

PLUNKY AND ONENESS OF JUJU Electric Juju Nation / Keep It Moving **N.A.M.E. Brand Record Company** 1984

ROY AYERS QUARTET All Blues 2 **Columbia** 1969

REVERIE Watch The Skies **Encounter Records** 1983

SAHIB SHIHAB + GILSON UNIT La Marche Dans Le Désert **Futura Records** 1972
Photography by Jean-Claude Planchet

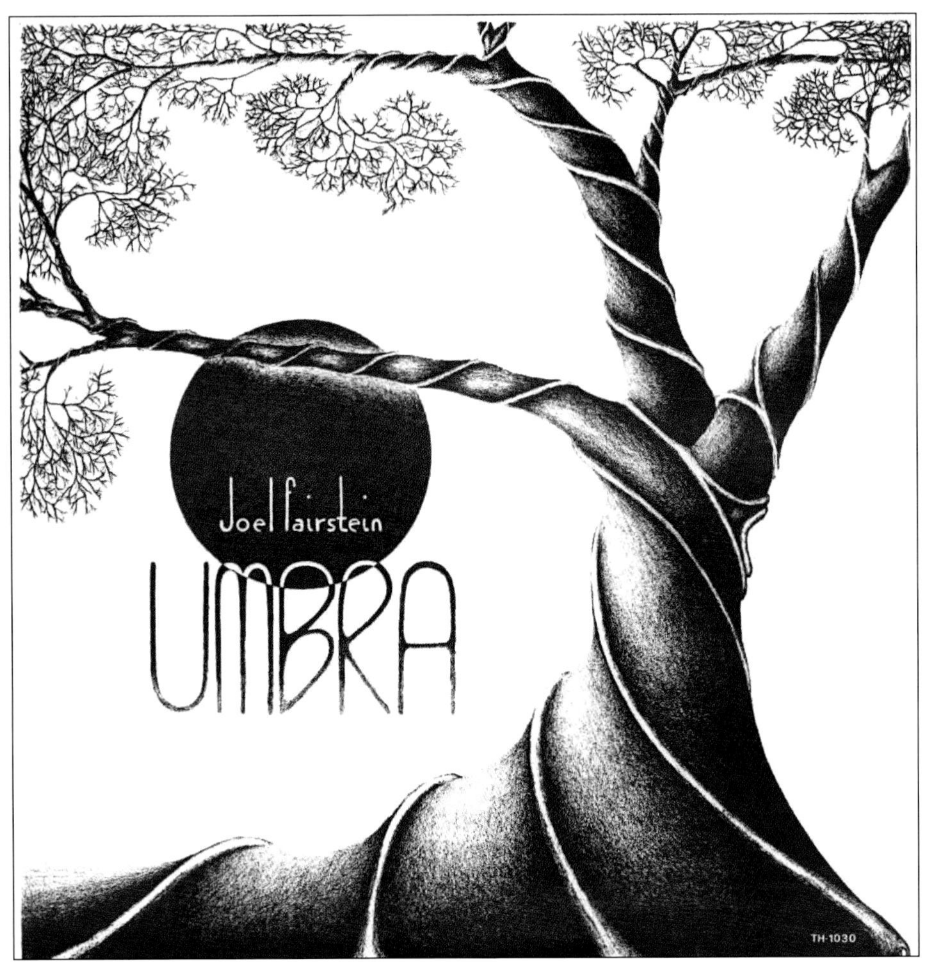

JOEL FAIRSTEIN Umbra **Thunderhead Records** 1978
Artwork Design Danny Hill **Art Direction** John Fairstein

MUSIC INC. Strata East Records 1971

RUDOLPH JOHNSON The Second Coming **Black Jazz Records** 1973 **Cover Art** Bud Doty **Photography and Concept by** Dorothy Tanous

MAL WALDRON

TOKYO REVERIE

MAL WALDRON Tokyo Reverie **Victor RCA Records** 1970

LEROY JENKINS The Legend Of Ai Glatson **Black Saint Records** 1978
Cover Artwork by "Gigi" Barbieri **Photography by** Giuseppe Pino

BLACK GIPSY
ARCHIE SHEPP
CHICAGO BEAU
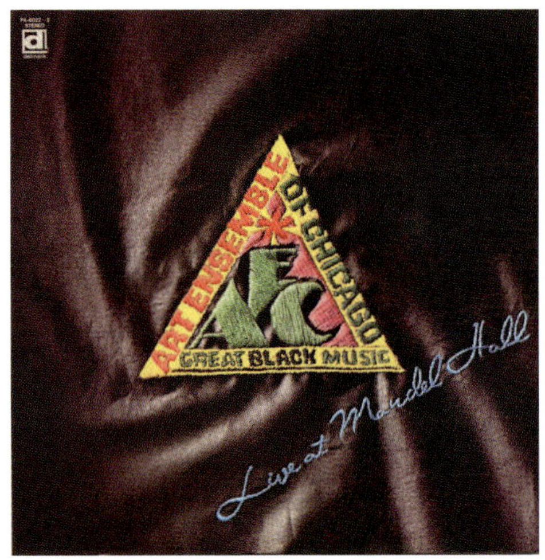
ART ENSEMBLE OF CHICAGO
AEC
GREAT BLACK MUSIC
Live at Mandel Hall

SIDNEY POITIER
READS
POETRY OF THE BLACK MAN

Julius Hemphill
Sackville 3014/15
A Two Record Set

STEREO·STEREO·STEREO·STEREO·STEREO·STEREO·STEREO·STEREO
THE TRANCE
BOOKER ERVIN

STEREO
max roach
members, don't git weary.
ATLANTIC

BASICALLY
BILL BELL
To Life & Love

CARLOS FRANZETTI
GrafiTTi

Live at Nemu Jazz Inn ·1
Bartz · Henderson · Connors
Dance of Magic

MOD LIT
Bethlehem Progressive Ensemble
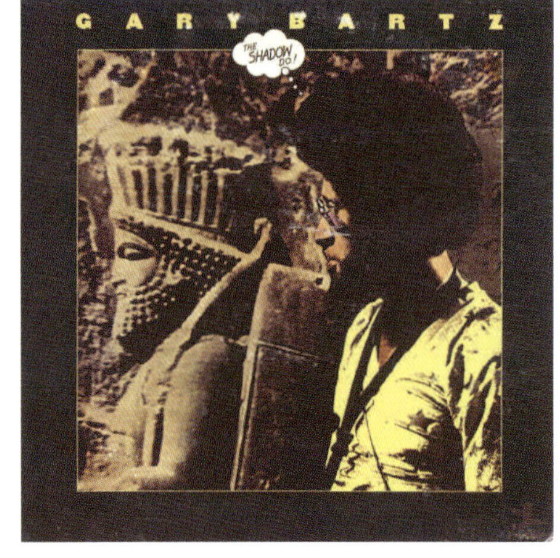
G A R Y B A R T Z
THE SHADOW DO!

KENYA
COALITION
Birth

DEDICACION
LYMAN WOODARD
ORGANIZATION

BASS CONTRA BASS
LISLE ATKINSON
Richard Wyands · Paul West · Al Harewood · Karen Atkinson

BAYETÉ UMBRA ZINDIKO · SEEKING OTHER BEAUTY
Prestige

AMBIANCE
INTO A NEW JOURNEY

Lord Shepherd Evidence For Real
Verline Records

quartet
New Steps
featuring
JOHN GILMORE

ANTHONY ORTEGA / NEW DANCE!
REVELATION
REV-M-3
featuring bassist
CHUCK DOMANICO

THE NEW YORK
BASS VIOLIN CHOIR
DIRECTED BY BILL LEE
basses:
LISLE ATKINSON
RON CARTER
RICHARD DAVIS
MICHEAL FLEMING
MILT HINTON
SAM JONES
BILL LEE
percussion:
SONNY
BROWN
guest artist:
GEORGE COLEMAN
and
HAROLD MABERN
performing excerpts from
"BABY SWEETS"
a narrative folk, jazz opera
written by Bill Lee and
Sonny Brown
STRATA-EAST

NATHEN PAGE
PAGE 1

NATURE'S
CONSORT

BYARD LANCASTER
Documentation:
The End of a Decade

THE ELEPHANT TROT DANCE - KHALIQ AL-ROUF & SALAAM
RECORDS
NQ3404
STEREO

Walt Dickerson
To My Queen
NEW JAZZ

ARCHIE SHEPP MEETS
KAHIL EL'ZABAR'S
RITUAL TRIO
«CONVERSATIONS»

THE
STRATUS
SEEKERS
GEORGE RUSSELL
SEPTET
RIVERSIDE
RLP 412

DAVID HOLLAND QUARTET / CONFERENCE OF THE BIRDS
DAVID HOLLAND
SAM RIVERS
ANTHONY BRAXTON
BARRY ALTSCHUL

Key To Nowhere
BROTHER AH
AND THE
SOUNDS OF AWARENESS

Faces of Jazz
MEDITATION

Nathan Davis
Suite for Dr. Martin Luther King, Jr.

Jackie McLean &
The Cosmic Brotherhood
New York Calling

PAUL JEFFREY QUINTET Electrifying Sounds of the... **Savoy Records** 1968

CHARLES MOFFETT 'The Gift' **Savoy Records** 1969
Cover Artwork by Charles Moffett

BLACK SAINT

Black Saint was established by Italian journalist and music critic, Giacomo Pellicciotti, with the help of Swiss financiers, in Rome, Italy in 1975. Black Saint released solely improvised, experimental, free and avant-garde jazz music of a very high standard.

Through his journalistic connections, Pellicciotti first travelled to New York to record albums by Richard Muhal Abrams, Don Pullen, Frank Lowe and many other members of the avant-garde/loft jazz community, recording them all at Generation Sound Studios in the city. These became early releases on the label. Subsequent releases were usually recorded in Paris and Milan, as well as New York. The first two releases were Billy Harper's 'Black Saint', and Archie Shepp's 'Sea of Faces'. Pellicciotti soon gathered together a highly credible catalogue that included new music by Steve Lacy, Don Cherry, Hamiet Bluett, Anthony Braxton, Lester Bowie, Max Roach, Julius Hemphill and more. Few American record companies could match this creative output. Pellicciotti continued to work as a journalist interviewing many artists including Keith Jarrett and Miles Davis.

In 1978, he handed the label over to producer Giovanni Bonandrini. The following year Bonandrini launched Soul Note, sister label to Black Saint. Both labels continued to release high quality music from the A-Class of the American avant-garde. In 1993, Giovanni Bonandrini passed both labels on to his son, Flavio, who continued to produce and run the label until 2008 when they were sold to C.A.M, a Rome based company who began to reissue the catalogue on CD.

BILL DIXON IN ITALY Volume One **Soul Note Records** 1980
Cover Artwork by Pick Up Studios **Photography by** Renzo Chiesa

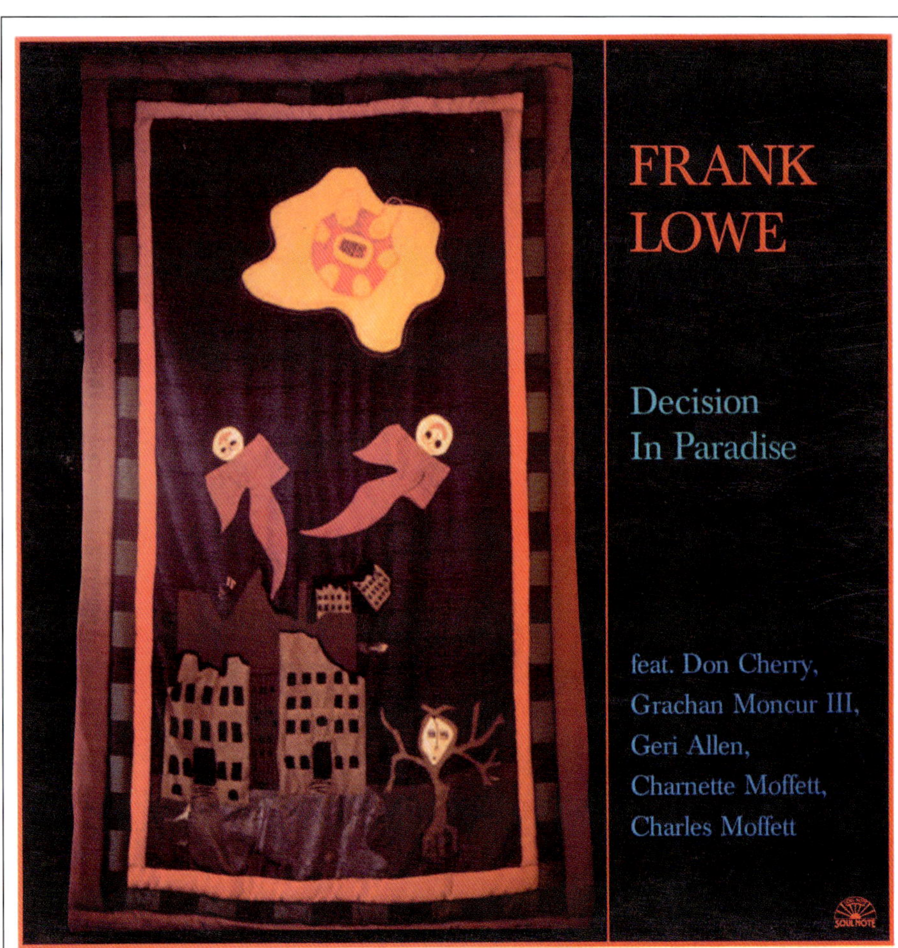

FRANK LOWE Decision In Paradise **Soul Note Records** 1985
Cover Artwork by Niridan **Cover Textile by** Carmen Lowe **Photography by** Alan Nahigiani

BILLY BANG QUINTET Invitation **Soul Note Records** 1982
Cover Artwork by Pick Up Studios

FRANK LOWE The Flam **Black Saint Records** 1976
Cover Artwork by Gabriel Soulè

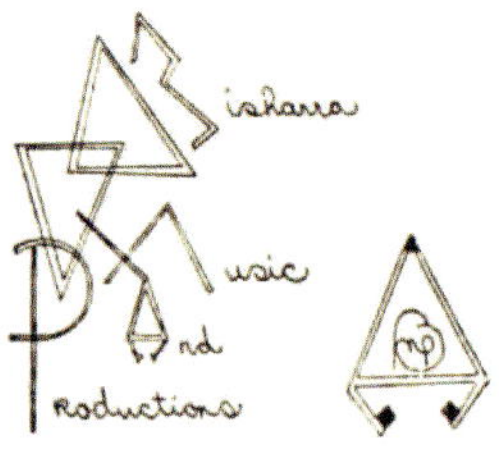

Abdul Wadud

— BY MYSELF —

Solo Cello

BR/101

ABDUL WADUD by Myself **Bishara Records** 1978
Cover Artwork and photography by Camille DeVaughn

12" SINGLE

NEW TRUTH

(Featuring Alphonso Bryant)

SARAI

(Black Flower)

NEW TRUTH FEATURING ALPHONSO BRYANT Sarai (Black Flower)

MAX ROACH HIS CHORUS AND ORCHESTRA It's Time **Impulse! Records** 1972 **Cover Artwork by** Robert Flynn

NIKKI GIOVANNI AND THE NEW YORK COMMUNITY CHOIR Truth Is On Its Way **Right On Records** 1971
Cover Artwork by Ronald Lucas **Photography by** George Frederick Wilson

MICHAEL WHITE The Land Of Spirit And Light **Impulse! Records** 1973
Cover Artwork by Carl Ramsay

ECM

The Third Decade

ART ENSEMBLE OF CHICAGO

ART ENSEMBLE OF CHICAGO The Third Decade **ECM Records** 1985
Cover Artwork by Roscoe E Mitchell **Design by** Barbara Wojirsch

PRINCE
FEATURING
WEBSTER
LASHA
ARMSTRONG
VOCALS
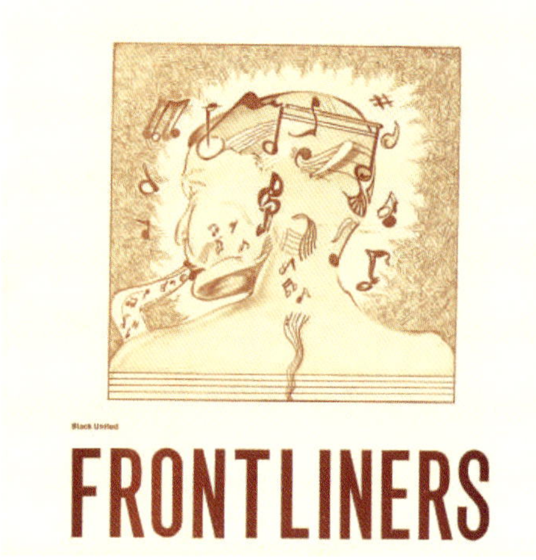
FRONTLINERS

the errol parker experience
graffiti
Sahara

Horacee Arnold
Tribe

CALVIN KEYS
CRISS CROSS

WILDFLOWERS 1
THE NEW YORK LOFT JAZZ SESSIONS
DOUGLAS
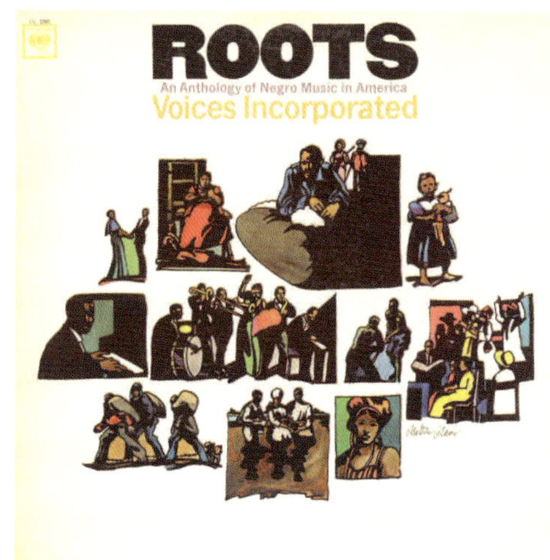
ROOTS
An Anthology of Negro Music in America
Voices Incorporated

trip to the orient
ronnie mathews

ANTHONY BRAXTON
FOUR COMPOSITIONS (QUARTET) 1984

FREE SPIRITS
MARY LOU WILLIAMS TRIO
SteepleChase SCS-1043 Stereo

ART ENSEMBLE OF CHICAGO
LIVE AT
MONTREUX JAZZ FESTIVAL
KABALABA

"In This World"
BY BILLY WOOTEN AND SPECIAL FRIENDS
featuring
STEVE WEAKLEY
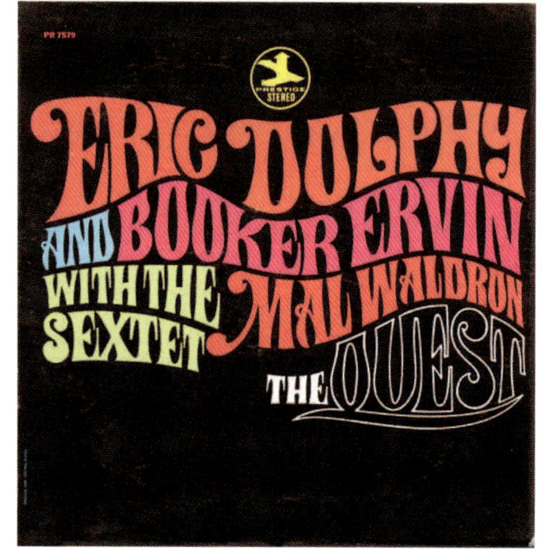
ERIC DOLPHY
AND BOOKER ERVIN
WITH THE MAL WALDRON SEXTET
THE QUEST

Ornette Coleman
The Art of The Improvisers

CHICAGO JAZZ ROCK
with gus giordano

REVOLUTIONARY ENSEMBLE
Leroy Jenkins
Sirone
Jerome Cooper

HORACE SILVER
Music To Ease Your Disease

GREG ADAMS KOOLIN OUT

Poum!

The Larry Douglas Alltet • Dedications

Wendell Harrison
Dreams Of A Love Supreme

THE ELECTRIC JAZZ OF GUS GIORDANO
THE JOHNNY FRIGO SEXTET

John Blair
MYSTICAL SOUL

SAM RIVERS
THE QUEST

Barry Wedgle
Jay Clayton
Jerry Granelli
Collin Walcott
Paul McCandless
Kake

ANOTHER GALAXY
THE GARY WILSON TRIO
STEREO

FROM RAG TIME
TO NO TIME
BEAVER HARRIS
THE 360 DEGREE
MUSIC EXPERIENCE

Earth Base One
NO COVER

ECM 1026 ST

STANLEY COWELL TRIÒ ILLUSION SUITE

STANLEY COWELL TRIO Illusion Suite **ECM Records** 1973
Cover Artwork by Grace Williams

Family

and

Friends

Hilton Felton

HILTON FELTON Family and Friends **Hilton's Concept Inc** c. 1982
Photography by Paul Fowlkes

HENRY GRIMES TRIO The Call **ESP Records** 1966
Cover Artwork by Stal Promotions **Photography by** Ray Gibson

NATHAN DAVIS Faces Of Love **Tomorrow International Inc Records** 1983
Cover Artwork by Gina Landis

REBIRTH

It seems obvious to state that the lineage of radical jazz music never ended. However the demise of record manufacturing, caused by the arrival of the compact disc, meant that the music did cease to exist on vinyl. Or nearly did. This technological shift caused the march of history to press pause.

No one could play, or listen to, or look at, for instance, Sun Ra's 'Nubians of Plutonia' if they did not already own a copy and still owned a record player. They could maybe try and track down a second-hand copy – remember life before Discogs! Originally released on Ra's own El Saturn Records in 1969, artfully re-released by Impulse in 1974, the album was never released on compact disc and remained out-of-print on vinyl for more than 25 years. Crazy, no? Musicians and music lovers wanting to study their music history encountered a void.

Two more new technological shifts changed this situation in a positive way. The first was the arrival of streaming – suddenly it was all there, nearly every piece of music you could ever want to hear. The second was the economic model-defying renaissance of vinyl as a format. As its slow rise from the ashes continues, more and more lost albums from this period are now reissued, most having been hidden for the last 50 years.

As a consequence, artists whose musical work had essentially been lost to the world were able to experience a renaissance from new younger fans. At the same time a new generation of artists are growing up now well-versed in this temporarily lost history, and choose to continue the exploratory path of jazz first travelled by John Coltrane and others. Many of these artists are releasing their music independently, outside of the mainstream. They are also focussed on those same ideas of self-determination, integrity and spiritual centredness that pumped through the veins of the original jazz artists featured in this book.

As all these phenomena occurred at the same time, this section is a snap-shot of all three – the renaissance of first-generation artists, the reissuing of long-lost musical artefacts, and a new generation artists who, with the same ethos, continue on the journey to enlightenment.

DAMON LOCKS BLACK MONUMENT ENSEMBLE Where Future Unfolds **International Anthem Recording Company** 2019 **Design by** Damon Locks

SADAKA Premonition **Jazzman Records** 2015 **Photography by** Emmanuel Nado

THEON CROSS Intra-I **New Soil** 2022 **Photography by** Ian Hippolyte

WAYNE DAVIS s/t **Strut** 2022 (Original Black Fire Records 1976) **Artwork by** Muzi Nubiatic

COMPASS Compass Rises **Frederiksberg Records** 2022 (Original Schoolhouse Productions 1973) **Design by** Barbara Lynch

BRAHJA s/t **RR GEMS** 2019 **Cover Artwork by** Hanz Mambo **Photography by** Isaac Rosenthal **Layout by** Ilja Tulit

KAMASI WASHINGTON The Epic **Brainfeeder** 2015 **Cover Artwork by** Patrick Henry Johnson, Kenturah Davis & Amoni Washington

IDRIS ACKAMOOR & THE PYRAMIDS Afro Futuristic Dreams **Strut Records Illustration by** David Alabo **Graphic Design by** Matt Thorne

SIRONE Artistry **Moved-By-Sound** 2022 **Photography by** Gösta Peterson

THE COLLECTIVE Idrissa's Dream **Strut** 2022 **Design by** Matt Thame

SOUTHERN UNIVERSITY JAZZ ENSEMBLE The Southern University Jazz Ensemble Goes To Africa With Love **Now-Again Records** 2023

MALIK'S EMERGING FORCE ART TRIO Time And Condition **Moved by Sound** 2022 **Photography by** Allah Shabazz & Mahasin Safee

FITZ GORE Soundmusication **Sonorama Records** 2022 **Cover Artwork by** Bernd Hagemann

ANDY HAY Polaris **Self-released** 2024 **Cover Artwork by** Andy Hay

WILBUR NILES AND THRUST Thrust Too **We Are Busy Bodies** 2023 (Original Tinkertoo Records1980)

ROLAND HAYNES JR. & PHENIX Mind Games **Athens Of The North** 2024 **Design by** Andrew Symington

MILFORD GRAVES & DON PULLEN Nomo **Superior Viaduct** 2023 **(Original SRP Records 1967) Design & Photography by** Roy DeCarava

MUSH TONE ENSEMBLE Walking On The Grass **RR GEMS** 2023

ORGANIC PULSE ENSEMBLE Oppression Is Nine Tenths Of The Law **RR GEMS** 2025 **Cover Artwork by** Agnes Horneij

ANGEL BAT DAWID & THE BROTHERHOOD Live **Intergalactic Mantra Recording Co.** 2021 **Design & Layout by** Craig Hansen

WILLIAM PARKER Mayam Space Station **AUM Fidelity** 2021 **Artwork & Design by** William Mazza Studio

PAT PATRICK AND THE BARITIONE SAXOPHONE RETINUE Sound Advice **Art Yard Records** 2015

VELS TRIO YELLOW Ochre **Total Refreshment Centre** 2017 **Cover Artwork by** Raymundo Wong

ROY BROOKS & THE IMPROVISATIONAL SPHERE Live At Lelli's **Sagittarius A-Star** 2011

EZRA COLLECTIVE Juan Pablo: The Philosopher **Enter The Jungle Records** 2017

NAT BIRCHALL Mysticism Of Sound **Ancient Archive Of Sound** 2020 **Cover Artwork & Photography by** Nat Birchall

MILFORD GRAVES WITH ARTHUR DOYLE & HUGH GLOVER Children of the Forest **Black Editions Archive** 2023 **Photography by** Val Wilmer

ANDY HAY Many Rivers **Self Released** 2023 **Hand-painted & hand-written Artwork by** Andy Hay

BROTHER AHH Move Ever Onward **Manufactured Recordings** 2016 (Original Divine Records 1975) **Design by** Dennis Critchlow

TED COLMAN BAND Taking Care Of Business **P-Vine Records** 2021 (Original JRS Records 1980) **Design by** T. Coleman

ORNETTE COLEMAN, JORDAN MCLEAN, AMIR ZIV, ADAM HOLZMAN New Vocabulary **System Dialing Records** 2014 **Cover Artwork by** Michelle Bothe

ROMAN NORFLEET & BE PRESENT ART GROUP Roman Norfleet & Be Present Art Group **Mississippi Records** 2023

ISACH SKEIDSVOLL Dance to Summon **Ultraääni** 2023
Cover Artwork by Arsi Keva **Photography by** Peder Skeidsvoll

ALAN BRAUFMAN Valley Of Search **P-Vine** 2020 (Original India Navigation 1975) **Cover Artwork by** Tamadah

INFINITE SPIRIT MUSIC Live Without Fear **Jazzman** 2018 (Original Ancient Africa Records 1980) **Cover Artwork by** Adebayo

KAMASI WASHINGTON Heaven and Earth **Young Turks** 2018
Art Direction by Kamasi Washington **Photography by** Mike Park

ABDULLAH SAMI Peace Of Time **Spiritmuse Records** 2019 (Original Abdullah Sami Records 1978)

PAT PATRICK AND THE BARITONE SAXOPHONE RETINUE Sound Advice **Art Yard Records** 2015

MURIEL GROSSMANN Natural Time **Dreamlandrecords** 2021

HIKIMA (YUSEF A. LATEEF) CREATIVITY
Key System Recordings 2019

THE COMET IS COMING Channel The Spirits **Test Pressing** 2016/7

ILL CONSIDERED Balm **New Soil** 2025
Cover Artwork by Vincent De Boer

MALEEM MAHMOUD GHANIA WITH PHAROAH SANDERS The Trance of Seven Colors **Zehara** 2019 **Cover Artwork by** Bernd Hagemann

NAT BIRCHALL Afro Trane 2022

NAT BIRCHALL The Infinite **Ancient Archive of Sound** 2023
Cover Image by Janice Wong **Design & Layout by** Nat Birchall

FITZ GORE & THE TALISMEN Soundnitia **Sonorama Records** 2021

THE CREATIVE ARTS ENSEMBLE Kaeef Ruzadun Presents
Creative Arts Records 2019

SHABAKA African Culture **Impulse!** 2022
Photography by Gareth Jarvis

DON CHERRY & OKAY TEMIZ Music For Turkish Theater 1970
CAZ PLAK 2024

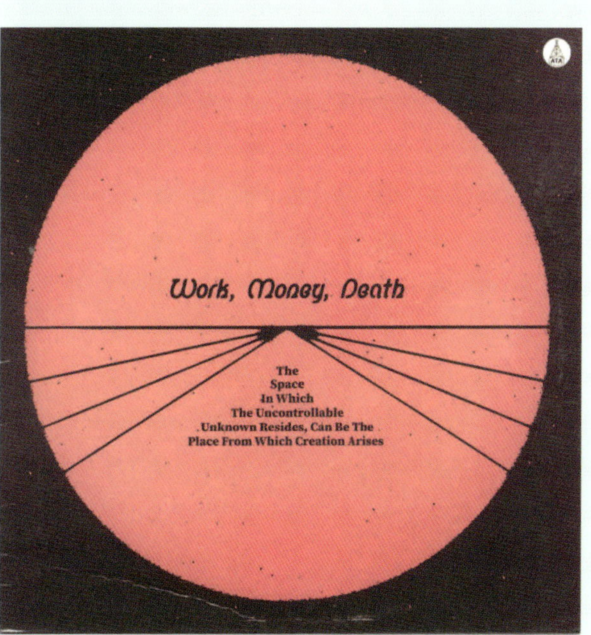

WORK, MONEY, DEATH The Space In Which The Uncontrollable Unknown Resides, Can Be The Place From Which Creation Arises **ATA Records** 2021 **Cover Artwork** Endless Studio